365 DAYS OF
INSTANT POT
RECIPES

NEW EDITION 2017

EMMA KATIE

Check out more books by Emma Katie at:
www.amazon.com/author/emmakatie

Contents

Breakfast Recipes

Soup, Broth and Chowder Recipes

Main courses

Appetizers and side dishes

Desserts

Yogurt recipes

Sauces

1 INTRODUCTION

Dear reader,

I would like to congratulate you for grabbing this book. This book has relevant information about the Instant pot and a great collection of various 365 recipes.

In the busy world as we are all living in on, having spare time is a big plus. The spare time you have is valuable and we appreciate your time. Therefore we have created this cookbook in order to give you healthy and nutritious meals that will not take all your time.

The easiest thing you can do is to go out and buy some junk food or grab some meals from a fine dine restaurant, but in such cases, you will need to spend a lot of money. Besides money, you must ask yourself how healthy those meals are?

Are you aware that French fries or fish sticks are fried in same oil that is used many times? As you can see, this is not a healthy option, maybe fast, but not good for you.

So, what is the solution?

The solution for these issues is in the homemade cooking from scratch. With our recipes that you can prepare in Instant pot, you will be able to eat healthy food while spending minimum time over the kitchen counter. The other benefits include the fact that you are the one that combines ingredients, so if you are not a fan of onion or garlic, you can simply avoid them. This is not something you can have in restaurant meals or store-bought meals.

After reading this book you will be able to create even some of your own staple dishes.

We have compiled best possible recipes in breakfast, soups, main courses, appetizers, side dishes, and desserts category, but we did not stop there. Since Instant pot allows you to create yogurt and sauces, we have tossed a few recipes for each of mentioned categories.

Thank you again for grabbing this book and we are sure you will love each of the recipes.

BENEFITS OF INSTANT POT

Fast cooking

Instant pot uses pressure to cook food and instead of cooking beans for 3 hours, you can have beans soup or bean chili ready in 45 minutes. This means you will not have to stand over the kitchen counter and check the doneness of beans because with the Instant pot you will always have perfectly cooked beans and legumes.

Preserves nutrients

Since food is steamed in Instant pot, most valuable vitamins and minerals are not destroyed, unlike with the classic cooking methods. Researchers have shown that when cooking with pressure, heat is evenly distributed, it all cooks at the same time, so no need for extension cooking. Also, with the Instant pot, you do not have to add water in order to prevent food burning.

Saves energy

Instant pot is built in such way that it does not require gas or electric stove to cook for longer periods. With slow cooker option in Instant pot, you may cook your food for a longer period, but with small use of energy. Statistics show that Instant pot saves energy up to 70% that the other cooking appliances and methods.

Kills harmful microorganisms

The Instant pot uses pressure cooking and temperatures higher that boiling water, which is effective in killing microorganisms. Therefore, Instant pot ca be used as a sterilizer for baby bottles and jam pots. When speaking about harmful microorganisms, most people think about chicken and salmonella. Unfortunately, many ignore mycotoxins from the corn and beans. With high pressure cooking these microorganisms that may cause even liver cancer, a safe environment is created and therefore foods from the Instant pot is completely safe to consume.

Safe to use

Many think that Instant pot is dangerous and that it may explode. This is completely false and with proper use, if Instant pot you will only experience positive things. The Instant pot is easy and simple to use and just read your manual before operating.

Cheap

Yes, the Instant pots are cheap although you may think otherwise. Instant pot is an appliance with different options; it can be used for stewing, as a rice cooker, as a yogurt maker, as a pressure cooker, as a slow cooker, as a steamer, and an option to keep the food warm. If you would buy all these appliance one by one, you would go much over the Instant pot price.

As you can see, the Instant pot has many benefits and if you do not own one, now it is the time.

Breakfast Recipes

SAUSAGE FRITTATA

Preparation time: 5 minutes   Cooking time: 15 minutes   Servings: 6

Ingredients:

1 lb. Italian Sausage
10 eggs, beaten
½ cup milk
1 teaspoon black pepper

1/2 teaspoon salt
2 tablespoons butter
2 cups Cheddar cheese, shredded

Directions:

Pour water into the Instant Pot and add a wire rack.

Coat the insides of a baking dish with butter.

Into a bowl, beat the eggs, and then add the sausage, milk, black pepper, salt, and cheese.

Carefully dump the mixture into the buttered baking dish then place the dish on top of the wire rack. Close the lid, and select the "Steam" function and "Adjust" up to 15 minutes.

Use a natural pressure release and serve while still hot.

COCONUT OATS

Preparation time: 5 minutes   Cooking time: 10 minutes   Servings: 4

Ingredients:

1 cup steel cut oats
1/2 cup unsweetened coconut flakes
1 pinch of salt

2 cups water
1 ¼ cups coconut milk
3 tablespoons sugar

Directions:

Toast the coconut flakes by adding it into the Instant Pot, then select the "Sauté" button and cook for 6 minutes.

Once the coconut flakes start to become a little brown, remove half of them and set them aside for the topping, then add the 1 cup steel cut oats into the Instant Pot to toast as well.

Cook the coconut flakes and oats for 3-5 minutes again using "Sauté". Add 1 cup coconut milk.

Add remaining ingredients and stir.

Press "Cancel" to stop "Sauté" then close the lid and press "manual" to choose 2 minutes and also select the "High Pressure" setting.

Once the 2 minutes are over, release pressure naturally.

Serve warm, topped with remaining milk.

Egg Breakfast Muffins

Preparation time: Cooking time: Servings: 4

Ingredients:

6 slices precooked bacon, diced   1/4 teaspoon lemon pepper seasoning
1 green onion, sliced and diced   4 eggs
4 tablespoons cheddar cheese, shredded   2 cups water

Directions:

Add 2 cups of water and a steamer basket into the Instant Pot.
Beat the eggs and lemon pepper.
Divide the green onion, bacon and cheese over 4 silicon muffin cups.
Then pour the beaten eggs evenly into every cup and use a fork to stir the mixture.
Place the muffins into steamer basket and lock the lid.
Select "Manual" and "High pressure." Set the timer to 10 minutes. Wien the beep sounds,
wait for 3 minutes then quick release the pressure.
Serve immediately.

Hardboiled Eggs

Preparation time: 5 minutes   Cooking time: 10 minutes   Servings: 4

Ingredients:

8 eggs   4 cups water

Directions:

Fill your pot with 4 cups of water and insert the eggs into a steamer basket and place it above the water.
2secure the lid and select the "Steam" function. Use the default time of 10 minutes, then allow a natural release of 5 minutes.
Use the quick-release method to release any remaining pressure then open the cooker.
Transfer the eggs to cold water and leave for 10 minutes. Peel and serve after.

Apple Oats Crisp

Preparation time: 5 minutes   Cooking time: 30 minutes   Servings: 4

Ingredients:

1/3 cup melted butter   1 tablespoon lemon juice
1/2 teaspoon salt   4 cups apples, peeled and diced
1 teaspoon cinnamon
1/2 cup brown sugar
1/3 cup flour
1 cup quick cooking oats

Directions:

Sprinkle the lemon juice over the apples to prevent browning.

In a bowl, combine and mix well the oats, salt, butter, brown sugar, flour, and cinnamon.

Arrange alternating layers of the oat and apple mixture in a buttered bowl that will fit into the Instant Pot. Cover it with aluminum foil

Place a wire rack inside the pot then add water, around 2 cups.

Select Porridge option and cook for 30 minutes. Perform a natural pressure release.

Serve after.

POTATO, TOMATO, AND EGGS CASSEROLES

Preparation time: 5 minutes   Cooking time: 10 minutes   Servings: 4

Ingredients:

4 eggs
1 onion, thinly sliced
1 cup baby spinach, chopped
2 carrots, thinly sliced
2 medium potatoes, peeled, thinly sliced

2 tomatoes, sliced
½ teaspoon salt
4 tablespoons butter
1 teaspoon black pepper
2 cups water

Directions

Crack eggs in a bowl and beat for 1 minute. Season with salt and pepper.

Grease a baking pan with butter. Add the carrots, potatoes, tomatoes, and pour over the eggs.

Fill your Instant pot with water, and place in the trivet. Place baking pan on trivet and cover with lid. Select the Manual cook mode and cook the eggs for 10 minutes. Use a natural pressure release.

Serve and enjoy.

ZUCCHINI FRITTATA

Preparation time: 5 minutes   Cooking time: 10 minutes   Servings: 4

Ingredients:

4 eggs
1 large zucchini
1 onion, chopped
1/2 teaspoon thyme, chopped

1/4 teaspoon salt
1/4 teaspoon white pepper
2 tablespoons olive oil

Directions:

Cut zucchini into thin strips and place aside. Crack eggs in a medium bowl and whisk with fork for 1 minute.

Add zucchini strips, onion, thyme, salt, and pepper, mix well.

Add 3-4 cups of water into an instant pot and place a trivet or stand in it.

Now spray a medium sized baking dish with olive oil, transfer eggs mixture into pan and place on the trivet.

Cover pot with lid and let to cook on manual mode for 10 minutes.

Serve hot and enjoy.

Egg filled avocado

Preparation time: 5 minutes   Cooking time: 15 minutes   Servings: 2

Ingredients:

2 eggs
1 avocado, pitted, halved
1 pinch salt

1 pinch black pepper
2 tablespoons olive oil

Directions:

Spray instant pot with oil.
Place avocados in instant pot and crack eggs into each avocado hole.
Sprinkle salt and pepper.
Cover with lid and leave to cook for 15 minutes on pressure cook mode.
Serve and enjoy.

Eggs and bread

Preparation time: 5 minutes   Cooking time: 5 minutes   Servings: 4

Ingredients:

4bread slices
4 eggs

1 pinch salt
2 tablespoons olive oil

Directions:

Place a cuter at the center bread and cut it to make a round hole. Repeat same for all bread slices.
Spray instant pot with oil.
Place bread slices in instant pot and crack eggs into it. Do for all slices. Sprinkle with salt.
Cover with lid and leave to cook for 5 minutes on pressure cook mode.
Serve while still hot.

Cheese omelette

Preparation time: 5 minutes   Cooking time: 5 minutes   Servings: 2

Ingredients:

2 eggs, whisked
1 teaspoon garlic powder
1/4 teaspoons salt
1/2 teaspoon black pepper
1/2 cup parmesan cheese, shredded
1/2 cup mozzarella cheese, shredded
3 tablespoons butter

Directions:

In eggs add mozzarella and parmesan cheese, season with salt, garlic, and pepper.
Melt butter in instant pot on sauté mode.
Pour eggs mixture and spread all over evenly. Let to cook for 2-3 minutes on one side then flip it.
Cook for 1-2 minutes and then transfer to serving platter.
Serve hot.

Spinach Casserole

Preparation time: 5 minutes   Cooking time: 25 minutes   Servings: 4

Ingredients:

1 cup spinach, chopped
8 oz. cheddar cheese
8 oz. mozzarella cheese
1 onion, chopped
4 eggs, whisked

I yellow bell pepper, chopped
1/4 teaspoon salt
1/4 teaspoon black pepper
2 tablespoons olive oil

Directions:

In a bowl add eggs, spinach, mozzarella cheese, cheddar cheese, bell pepper, and onion, mix well.
Season with salt and pepper.
Grease instant pot with olive oil. Transfer spinach mixture to the instant pot and cover with lid.
Leave to cook for 25 minutes on slow cook mode.
Serve hot with bread.

Instant Granola

Preparation time: 5 minutes   Cooking time: 35 minutes   Servings: 4

Ingredients:

2 cups granola
1 cup dates, seeded, halved
1 cup milk
1/4 cup peanuts
1/2 cup coconut milk

1/4 cup coconut flakes
1 egg, whisked
1/4 cup brown sugar
1 pinch salt
2 tablespoons butter, melted

Directions:

Blend the dates and milk until smooth.
Now add brown sugar, granola, salt, butter, peanuts, and egg, mix to combine.
Transfer to greased instant pot and let to cook for 35 minutes on slow cook mode.
Serve and enjoy.

BLUEBERRY OATS

Preparation time: 5 minutes   Cooking time: 35 minutes   Servings: 4

Ingredients:

1 cup old-fashioned oats
1 cup blueberries
1 cup cream milk

1/4 cup caster sugar
4 tablespoons honey
2 tablespoons butter, melted

Directions:

Combine oats, cream milk, sugar, and butter in a bowl.
Transfer oats mixture to instant pot and place blueberries on top, cover with lid.
Let to cook on slow cook mode for 35 minutes.
Drizzle honey on top while serving.
Serve and enjoy.

EGGS AND POTATOES

Preparation time: 5 minutes   Cooking time: 8 minutes   Servings: 4

Ingredients:

2 potatoes, peeled, chopped
4 eggs, whisked
½ teaspoon chili powder
¼ teaspoon salt

¼ teaspoon cumin powder
¼ teaspoon cinnamon powder
¼ teaspoon black pepper
3 tablespoons olive oil

Directions:

Heat 2 tablespoons of oil in instant pot on sauté mode. Add eggs and cook for 1 minute. Flip and cook for 1 minute more.
Now transfer egg to a platter and let to cool. Crumble egg with folk.
Now add remaining oil and fry potatoes for 4-5 minutes.
Season with salt, chili powder, black pepper, cumin powder, and cumin powder.
Transfer crumbled egg and stir well.
Serve after.

SCRAMBLED EGGS

Preparation time: 5 minutes   Cooking time: 5 minutes   Servings: 4

Ingredients:

4 eggs, whisked
1/4 teaspoon salt
1 cup chicken broth
1/4 teaspoon black pepper

1/4 teaspoon dill, chopped
2 tablespoons olive oil

Directions:

Heat oil in instant pot on sauté mode and add whisked eggs. Scramble eggs with folk continuously and add chicken broth.

Season with salt and pepper.

When the chicken broth is dried out transfer egg scrambles to serving dish and top with dill.

Serve and enjoy.

$\mathcal{B}$REAKFAST PUDDING

Preparation time: 5 minutes   Cooking time: 20 minutes   Servings: 2

Ingredients:

1 cup mango, chunks
1 cup orange juice
1 pear, chopped

1 apple, chopped
1 cup milk

Directions:

In instant, pot add all ingredients and stir to combine. Lock and cook on low for 20 minutes.

Puree with an immersion blender and simmer for 5 minutes.

Serve after.

$\mathcal{O}$ATMEAL PANCAKES

Preparation time: 5 minutes   Cooking time: 10 minutes   Servings: 4

Ingredients:

1 cup oats
1 cup all-purpose flour
1/2 cup caster sugar
1/4 teaspoon baking soda
1/2 teaspoon baking powder
2 eggs

1 cup heavy milk
2 tablespoons sour cream
4 tablespoons honey
4 tablespoons butter
1 pinch salt

Directions:

Sift flour, sugar, baking powder, baking soda, salt, and place aside.

Beat eggs for 1 minute and add in milk, sour cream and mix well.

Add sifted flour mixture and oats, mix with spatula thoroughly.

Melt butter in instant pot. Ladle the batter in pot and spread in the form of Let to cook for 2-3 minutes on 1 side, then flip to the other side and let to cook till nicely brown.

Transfer to sewing platter and drizzle honey.

Top with fresh fruits.

Tomato Eggs

Preparation time: 5 minutes   Cooking time: 10 minutes   Servings: 2

Ingredients:

2 eggs, whisked
2 tomatoes, sliced
1 teaspoon garlic powder

1/4 teaspoons salt
1/2 teaspoon chili powder
3 tablespoons butter

Directions:

Melt butter in instant pot on Sauté mode.
Add eggs and speed all over. Let to cook for 1-2 minutes then flip to another side.
Place tomato slices and cover pot with lid, let to cook on pressure cooker mode for 10 minutes.
Season with salt and chili powder.
Serve immediately.

Quinoa Spinach Casserole

Preparation time: 5 minutes   Cooking time: 20 minutes   Servings: 6

Ingredients:

6 eggs

1 cup quinoa
2 cups baby spinach
1 cup milk or almond milk
1 cup sharp cheddar cheese, shredded

1 cup chicken broth
4 tablespoons olive oil
½ teaspoon salt
½ teaspoon black pepper

Directions:

Beat the eggs with salt and pepper in a bowl.
Combine the eggs with quinoa, baby spinach, cheddar cheese, chicken broth and stir well to combine.
Grease Instant pot with olive oil and transfer quinoa mixture into the pot.
Cover and cook on slow cook mode for 20 minutes.
Serve while still hot.

Chocolate Coconut Oatmeal

Preparation Time: 5 minutes   Cooking Time: 30 minutes   Servings: 4

Ingredients:

2 cup old fashioned oats
1 tablespoon cocoa powder
1 cup coconut milk
2 cups water
½ cup heavy cream

1 cup chocolate chips
¼ cup brown sugar
4 tablespoons honey
2 tablespoons butter

Directions:

In a medium bowl, combine the oats, water, cocoa powder, coconut milk, cream, chocolate chips and brown sugar.

Grease Instant pot with butter and transfer oat mixture into the pot.

Cover and cook on slow cook mode for 30 minutes.

Serve in a bowl, and drizzle with honey.

CHOCOLATE APPLE CRUMBLE

Preparation Time: 5 minutes   Cooking Time: 30 minutes   Servings: 6

Ingredients:

4 red apples, peeled, cored, sliced
2 cups granola
1 cup almond milk
½ cup brown sugar

4 tablespoons butter
½ teaspoon pumpkin pie spice
½ cup dark chocolate chips

Directions:

Combine apples with granola, chocolate chips, almond milk, brown sugar, and pumpkin spice.

Grease Instant pot with butter and transfer the apple mixture into the pot.

Select the Slow Cook mode and cook the crumble for 30 minutes.

Serve while still hot.

MANGO INSTANT POT CRUMBLE

Preparation Time: 5 minutes   Cooking Time: 20 minutes   Servings: 4

Ingredients:

1 cup fresh strawberries, chopped
1 cup mango, chopped
1 cup blanched almond flour
1 cup almond milk
½ cup brown sugar

¼ cup almonds, chopped
2 tablespoons butter
1 cup whipped coconut cream, to serve with

Directions:

Grease Instant pot with some butter.

Combine all ingredients in instant pot and lock the lid.

Set Instant pot on Slow Cook mode and cook for 20 minutes.

Serve the crumble in a bowl and top with whipped cream.

Apple Cinnamon Oatmeal

Preparation time: 5 minutes   Cooking time: 7 minutes   Servings: 4

Ingredients:

1 tablespoon brown sugar
1 red apple, chopped and peeled
2 ½ cups water
1 cup steel oats

3 tablespoons butter
¼ teaspoon salt
1 teaspoon Ceylon cinnamon

Directions:

Set the instant pot to Sauté option. Once warm add the butter and let it melt.
Add the remaining ingredients and give it a good stir.
Select manual and cook oats on a high pressure for 7 minutes.
Once the cycle is done, slowly release the pressure for about 10 minutes.
Serve while still hot.

French Toast from the Pot

Preparation time: 5 minutes   Cooking time: 15 minutes   Servings: 6

Ingredients:

2 tablespoon maple syrup
1 cup milk
3 eggs, whisked
1 teaspoon butter

1 ½ cups water
1 teaspoon sugar
3 cups cinnamon raisin bread, cubed
1 teaspoon vanilla paste

Directions:

Pour water in the instant pot and place in the trivet.
Grease the baking pan with butter.
In a large bowl, whisk the eggs, maple syrup, milk, vanilla, and maple syrup. Add the bread nd let it sit for 5 minutes. Transfer the bread into baking dish and place all in the pot.
Cook on manual for 15 minutes.
Once the cycle is over, use the quick pressure release, and carefully lift the pan out. Serve warm.

Egg Rice Pudding

Preparation time: 5 minutes   Cooking time: 7 minutes   Servings: 4

Ingredients:

¼ cup maple syrup
1 ½ cups egg nog
¼ teaspoon cinnamon
½ teaspoon nutmeg
½ teaspoon rum extract

½ vanilla paste
2 cups water
1 cup Arborio rice
¼ stick of butter

Directions:

Set up the instant pot to high. Once hot add the butter and melt.

Add in the cinnamon, nutmeg, rum extract, vanilla, water, and rice.

Lock the lid and set to a high pressure. Cook for 7 minutes. Once the cooking cycle is done, use a quick pressure release.

Stir in the maple syrup and the eggnog.

Serve after.

CINNAMON BREAD ROLLS

Preparation time:　　　　　　Cooking time:　　　　　　Servings: 6

Ingredients:

½ cup brown sugar

3 cups almond milk

4 eggs, whisked

2 teaspoon vanilla paste

½ teaspoon cinnamon

1 pinch salt

7 slices cinnamon bread, cubed

½ raisins or chopped dates

5 tablespoons melted butter

Caramel Sauce:

¾ cup brown sugar

¼ cup corn syrup

3 teaspoons heavy cream

2 tablespoons butter

1 pinch salt

2 teaspoons vanilla paste

½ cup toasted pecans

Directions:

In a bowl, stir the butter, sugar, almond milk, cinnamon, salt, eggs,

and vanilla. Add in the cubed bread and raisins. Place aside for 20 minutes.

Fill the pot with water and place in the trivet.

Transfer the bread mixture to baking dish and place in the Instant pot. Select the Manual and cook on high pressure for 20 minutes. Use a quick pressure release method.

Heat the oven to 350F and cook the bread rolls for 10 minutes or until the top is crumbly.

Meanwhile, prepare the caramel sauce; combine all ingredients, except the vanilla and pecans in an instant pot. Select the Saute. Lower the temperature a bit and cook until the sugar melts. Stir in the vanilla and pecans.

Once the bread is crumbly, slice it and serve with caramel sauce.

ITALIAN SAUSAGE FRITTATA

Preparation time: 5 minutes　　　　　　Servings: 4

Cooking time: 17 minutes

Ingredients:

½ cup cooked and crumbled Italian sausage

2 tablespoons sour cream

4 eggs, beaten

1 tablespoon

¼ cup cheddar cheese, shredded

Salt and pepper, to taste

Directions:

Pour 2 cups water in an Instant pot and place in the trivet.

Grease baking dish with butter.

In a bowl, whisk together the sour cream and eggs. Stir in the cheese and sausage and season with salt and pepper. Pour the egg mixture into prepared baking dish and place into instant pot.

Lock the lid and cook on low for 17 minutes. Use a quick pressure release and allow to cool for few minutes before serving.

Fast Egg muffin cups

Preparation time: 5 minutes   Cooking time: 9 minutes   Servings: 6 muffins

Ingredients:

4 eggs
¼ teaspoon lemon pepper seasoning
4 tablespoon Cheddar shredded cheese

1 spring onion, sliced
6 slices bacon, chopped

Directions:

Pour 2 cups of water Into the instant pot. Add in the steaming basket.

Whisk the eggs and lemon pepper in a bowl.

Divide the cheese, bacon, and spring onion between six silicone muffin molds.

Pour over the eggs and place the cups into steaming basket.

Select the Manual and cook the muffins on high pressure for 9 minutes.

Use a quick pressure release method.

Serve muffins while still hot.

Bulgur Breakfast Salad

Preparation time: 10 minutes   Cooking time: 6 minutes   Servings: 6

Ingredients:

1/3 cup olive oil
Juice from 2 lemons
3 celery ribs, chopped
2 red bell peppers, chopped
1 summer squash, cubed

4 cups water
2 tablespoons vegetable oil
2 teaspoons salt
2 cups bulgur, rinsed
Salt and pepper, to taste

Directions:

Combine the water, vegetable oil, salt, and bulgur in the instant pot.

Select the Manual and bring to a high pressure. Cook for 6 minutes and use a natural release method. Drain the bulgur and fluff with a fork.

Add the celery, bell pepper, and summer squash and stir to combine.

In a bowl, whisk the rest of the ingredients. Drizzle this over the salad and chill in the fridge until ready to serve.

CREAMY APRICOTS WITH HONEY

Preparation time: 5 minutes   Cooking time: 5 minutes   Servings: 4

Ingredients:

1 cup cream cheese or mascarpone cheese
2 tablespoons honey
1 teaspoon ground cinnamon
¼ teaspoon vanilla extract

2 tablespoons brown sugar
¼ cup water
¼ cup apple juice
8 pitted and halved apricots

Directions:

Combine all of the ingredients except the cream cheese and honey in an instant pot.
Lock the lid, and select Manual. Cook on low pressure for 5 minutes.
Use a natural pressure release and remove the apricots.
In a small bowl, cream the cheese and honey. Top each apricot with cheese before serving.

ALMOND BANANA LOAF

Preparation time: 5 minutes   Cooking time: 15 minutes   Servings: 1 loaf

Ingredients:

2 cups almond flour
1 teaspoon baking soda
3 ripe bananas, mashed
3 eggs

¼ cup olive oil
½ cup walnuts, chopped
Some butter, to grease loaf pan

Directions:

In a bowl, combine the almond flour, baking soda, mashed bananas, eggs, and olive oil.
Add half of the chopped walnuts. Brush the silicone loaf pan with some melted butter and pour in prepared batter. Sprinkle with remaining walnuts. Cover with aluminum foil.
Pour 2 ½ cups water in the instant pot and place in the steaming basket. Place the mold inside the basket and lock the lid.
Select the Steam mode and set the timer to 15 minutes. After the cycle is done, use a natural pressure release. Allow to cool before removing from the silicone mold and slicing.

FLUFFY FRUIT QUINOA

Preparation time: 5 minutes   Cooking time: 10 minutes   Servings: 4

Ingredients:

1 cup strawberries
½ cup sliced almonds
2 cups water
2 cup quinoa

½ teaspoon Ceylon cinnamon
½ teaspoon vanilla extract
1 pinch salt
2 tablespoons maple syrup

Directions:

Combine the almonds, water, quinoa, cinnamon, vanilla, salt, and maple syrup in an instant pot.
Select Manual and set the pressure to high. Cook for 10 minutes and use a quick pressure release after.
Open the pot and serve quinoa in a bowl. Top with strawberries before serving.

COCONUT VANILLA OATS

Preparation time: 5 minutes   Cooking time: 5 minutes   Servings: 4

Ingredients:

1 cup steel cut oats
2 teaspoons vanilla paste
½ cup coconut flakes
1 cup coconut milk

2 cups water
2 tablespoons brown sugar
1 teaspoon cinnamon

Directions:

Set the Instant pot to Saute and add in the coconut flakes. Let the warm for 5 minutes. Once the flakes are golden, remove 2/3 of the flakes. Pour in the coconut milk, vanilla, cinnamon, and brown sugar. Stir well and add the water and steel cut oats.

Select the Manual and cook on high pressure for 5 minutes. Use natural pressure release. Open the lid and serve oats in a bowl.

Top with reserved coconut flakes.

GERMAN SAUSAGE BREAKFAST CASSEROLE

Preparation time: 10 minutes   Cooking time: 15 minutes   Servings: 10

Ingredients:

1lb. German sausage, casing removed
30oz. hash browns, thawed
½ cup skim milk
6 onions, sliced into rings

½ cup cheddar cheese, shredded
1 cup mozzarella cheese, shredded
10 eggs, beaten
Salt and pepper, to taste

Directions:

Turn on the instant pot and select the Saute.

Place in the hash browns and top with crumbled sausage. Add layers of cheddar cheese, mozzarella, and onions.

In a bowl, whisk eggs with milk, salt, and pepper. Pour the eggs over previous ingredients and lock the lid. Select the Manual and cook on high pressure for 15 minutes.

Use a natural pressure release and allow to cool down before serving.

Breakfast Beef

Preparation time: 10 minutes   Cooking time: 20 minutes   Servings: 6

Ingredients:

1 onion, chopped
1lb. beef stew meat, cubed
10oz. broccoli florets
1tablespoon ground ginger

1 garlic clove, minced
½ cup bone broth
2 tablespoons fish sauce
Salt and pepper, to taste

Directions:

Take the instant pot and set it to "sauté" for 5 minutes.

Place the onions, ginger, fish sauce, bone broth, beef, salt, and pepper in instant pot.

Close the lid and press the "Meat Stew" feature on the Instant Pot. Let it cook for 20 minutes and then wait for it to release the pressure.

Open the lid and add the broccoli.

Put the lid back on and let it heat up alongside.

Let it sit for around 15 minutes.

Serve after and enjoy!

Banana Bread

Preparation time: 5 minutes   Cooking time: 30 minutes   Servings: 1 loaf

Ingredients:

2 bananas, mashed
1 cup plain flour
1 teaspoon cream of tartar
1 teaspoon baking powder
¼ cup ghee, melted
1/3 cup flour

1 teaspoon vanilla paste
1 egg, beaten
¾ cup sugar
1 teaspoon baking soda
½ cup almond milk

Directions:

In a bowl, whisk the liquid ingredients, including banana. In a separate bowl, whisk dry ingredients. Fold the liquid ingredients into the flour mixture and stir well to combine.

Pour 2 cups water in the instant pot and place in the trivet. Pour prepared mixture into silicone loaf mold and place the mold onto trivet.

Press "manual" and set the time to 30 minutes. Let the pressure release naturally.

Remove the banana bread from the pot and let it cool down for 1 hour

Once completely cooled, you can slice and serve.

Colored Sausages

Preparation time: 5 minutes   Cooking time: 20 minutes   Servings: 4

Ingredients:

1 red bell pepper, seeded, chopped
2 potatoes, diced
1 teaspoon ground garlic
1 teaspoon turmeric
1 pinch salt
½ teaspoon ground cumin

¼ teaspoon black pepper
1 cup baby spinach
5 button mushrooms, sliced
6oz. tofu cubed
1 package sausages

Directions:

Take the instant pot and press "Sauté"

Take the sausages and place them inside the Instant Pot. Let the sausages cook for 2 minutes.

Add the potatoes, red bell pepper, turmeric, salt, black pepper, tofu, mushrooms, spinach, ground cumin, and turmeric.

Select the Manual and cook for 20 minutes.

Let the pressure release naturally. Serve while still hot.

Coconut Lime Yogurt

Preparation time: 5 minutes   Cooking time: 11 hours   Servings: 4

Ingredients:

1 tablespoon gelatin
30oz. coconut cream
1 cup coconut milk

3 capsules probiotic
1 tablespoon lime juice

Directions:

Pour the milk in the instant pot. Press "Yogurt On the Instant Pot and let it
work away on the coconut milk You want it to be properly boiled.

Take out the coconut milk and place aside to cool. Place in the probiotic capsules.

Transfer the content into the pot again, add coconut cream, and press yogurt. Set it to Yogurt option and cycle for 11 hours. Once the cycle is done, stir in the lime juice, and gelatin. Chill the yogurt for 3 hours and serve after.

Bacon Egg Sandwich

Preparation time: 10 minutes   Servings: 4

Ingredients:

4 slices bacon

4 eggs

4 bread slices

Directions:

Take out the Instant Pot and set it to "sauté" for 5 minutes.

You will begin to cook the eggs separately in an oven.

You will place the bread inside the Instant Pot and let it sit Inside.

Add the egg and bacon on top

Set it aside for 10 minutes and it should be ready to go.

Enjoy!

Creamy coconut oats

Preparation time: 5 minutes   Cooking time: 2 minutes   Servings: 4

Ingredients:

½ cup of coconut flakes, unsweetened

2 cups of water

1 cup of oats

1 cup of coconut milk

2 tablespoons of brown sugar

1 pinch salt

1 cinnamon stick

Directions:

Toast the coconut in an Instant pot by selecting the Saute button.

You should stir the coconut frequently in order to make sure that there are no burning pieces.

Once the coconut starts to turn a light brown, you can then add the oats. Cook both of the ingredients for a few minutes. Stir in the milk, salt, brown sugar, and add the cinnamon stick. Lock the lid and cook on high pressure for 2 minutes.

Once the cooking process is complete, use the natural release method in order to release the pressure.

Serve after.

ALMOND QUINOA

Preparation time: 1 minutes   Cooking time: 1 minutes   Servings: 6

Ingredients:

1 ½ cups quinoa
2 ¼ cups almond milk
2 tablespoons maple syrup

½ teaspoon vanilla extract
¼ teaspoon cinnamon
1 pinch salt

Directions:

Combine all ingredients and transfer into the instant pot.

Close the lid of the Instant pot and select the Manual. Cook on high pressure for 1 minute. Use the natural pressure release method.

Serve while still hot with favorite topping.

CHICKEN PORRIDGE

Preparation time: 5 minutes   Cooking time: 15 minutes   Servings: 6

Ingredients:

1 cup basmati rice
1lb. chicken legs
5 cups chicken broth

4 cup water
1 tablespoon grated ginger
Green onion and pecan nuts, to serve with

Directions:

Place all the ingredients into the instant pot.

Turn on the porridge option and let it cook until the default countdown runs out.

Release the pressure naturally

Open up the lid and remove the chicken legs and just shred the meat.

Stir the meat into the rice and serve in bowls.

Top with green onions and pecan nuts.

Soup, Broth and Chowder Recipes

CREAMED CORN BASE

Preparation time: 5 minutes   Cooking time: 6 minutes   Servings: 4

Ingredients:

1 cup corn kernels
1 cup water
1 cup full fat milk

Salt and pepper
½ cup half and half

Directions:

Place all ingredients in the instant pot.

Select sauté mode and bring to a boil. Lock the lid and select manual button and cook on high pressure for 5-6 minutes.

Perform a natural pressure release and blend ingredients using an immersion blender.

Season with salt and pepper.

PRAWN STOCK

Preparation time: 10 minutes   Cooking time: 30 minutes   Servings: 10

Ingredients:

2 cups large prawns
1 large carrot
1 large onion
10 garlic cloves

1 celery stalk
15 whole peppercorns
6 cups water

Directions:

Select sauté mode on the pot and add the prawns, onion, celery, carrot and peppercorns.

Pour in the water and close the lid.

Select Pressure mode and cook on low pressure for 30 minutes.

Use a natural pressure release and strain the stock.

Serve with warm bread or use as a base for many dishes.

Seafood Stock

Preparation time: 5 minutes   Cooking time: 30 minutes   Servings: 10

Ingredients:

½ cup big prawns
½ cup clams
½ cup fish fillets (any fish)
½ cup mussels
1 large carrot

1 large onion
10 garlic cloves
1 stalk celery
15 whole peppercorns
6 cups water

Directions:

Select sauté mode on the instant pot and add all ingredients.
Select Pressure mode and cook on low pressure for 30 minutes.
Remove the pressure using a natural pressure release.
Strain the stock and serve while still hot with toasted bread or as a base for many dishes.

Saffron Prawn Stock

Preparation time: 5 minutes   Cooking time: 30 minutes   Servings: 10

Ingredients:

2 cups jumbo prawns
1 large carrot
1 red onion
10 garlic cloves

2 celery stalks
15 whole peppercorns
7-8 saffron strands
6 cups water

Directions:

Select sauté mode on the instant pot and add all ingredients.
Seal the lid, select pressure mode and cook on low pressure for 30 minutes
Use a natural pressure release to open the pot.
Strain the stock and serve while still hot or as a base for many dishes.

Leftover Turkey Stock

Preparation time: 5 minutes   Cooking time: 30 minutes   Servings: 10

Ingredients:

2 cups leftover turkey meat
1 large parsnip
1 large onion
1 head garlic, crushed
2 celery stalks
1 carrot

15 whole peppercorns
6 cups water

Directions:

Select sauté mode on the instant pot and add all ingredients.

Seal the lid, select pressure mode and cook on low pressure for 30 minutes

Use a natural pressure release to open the pot.

Strain the stock and serve while still hot with bread croutons or as a base for many dishes.

VEGETABLE BROTH

Preparation time: 5minutes   Cooking time: 30 minutes   Servings: 10

Ingredients:

2 large carrots
1 zucchini
6 sprigs parsley
1 large parsnip
1 large red onion

10 cloves garlic
2 celery stalks
15 whole peppercorns
6 cups water

Directions:

Select sauté mode on the instant pot and add all ingredients.

Seal the lid, select pressure mode and cook on low pressure for 30 minutes

Use a natural pressure release to open the pot.

Strain the stock and place aside. Puree the veggies using an immersion blender.

Stir the pureed vegetables into the stock and reheat altogether.

Serve after.

CLASSIC CHICKEN BROTH

Preparation time: 5 minutes   Cooking time: 30 minutes   Servings: 4

Ingredients:

1 chicken carcass
2 carrots
4 sprigs basil
1 parsnip
1 brown onion

6 garlic cloves
2 celery stalks
15 whole peppercorns
6 cups water

Directions:

Select sauté mode on the instant pot and add all ingredients.

Seal the lid, select pressure mode and cook on low pressure for 30 minutes

Use a natural pressure release to open the pot.

Strain the stock and serve while still hot or as a base for many dishes.

POTATO CORN CHOWDER

Preparation time: 5 minutes   Cooking time: 20 minutes   Servings: 6

Ingredients:

6 ears fresh corn
4 tablespoons butter
½ cup onion, chopped
3 cups water
1 lb. russet potatoes, peeled and halved
2 tablespoons dried parsley

2 tablespoons cornstarch
3 cups half-and-half
½ cup sharp cheddar cheese
¼ teaspoon cayenne pepper powder
Salt and freshly ground pepper, to taste

Directions:

Separate the corn kernels and keep them aside. Sauté onions in butter until soft. You will do this in your instant pot on Saute option. Add 3 cups water, potatoes, parsley, and corn kernels.

Lock the instant pot and select the Manual mode. Set the timer to 8 minutes.

When the timer beeps, turn off the pot and do a quick pressure release.

Leave the corn broth in the pot and place a steamer basket. Add potatoes, corn kernels, and select Pressure function. Cook for 4 minutes on high pressure. Use a quick pressure release.

Carefully remove the steamer basket and place the content aside.

Dissolve cornstarch in some water and stir in the corn broth.

Select Simmer and whisk the cornstarch into the soup. Simmer until it thickens. Stir in half-and-half, cayenne pepper, potatoes, and cheddar cheese. Adjust seasoning and serve while still hot.

PLAIN CORN CHOWDER

Preparation time: 10 minutes   Cooking time: 20 minutes   Servings: 6

Ingredients:

6 fresh corn ears
4 tablespoons butter
½ cup onion, chopped
3 cups water
2 tablespoons dried parsley

2 tablespoons cornstarch
3 cups half and half
¼ teaspoon cayenne pepper powder
Salt and pepper, to taste

Directions:

Separate the corn kernels and keep them aside.

Sauté onions in butter until soft. You will do this in your instant pot on Saute option.

Add 3 cups water, parsley, and corn kernels.

Lock the instant pot and select the Manual mode. Set the timer to 8 minutes.

When the timer beeps, turn off the pot and do a quick pressure release.

Dissolve cornstarch in some water and stir in the corn broth.

Select Simmer and whisk the cornstarch into the soup. Simmer until it thickens.

Stir in half-and-half and cayenne pepper. Adjust seasoning and serve while still hot.

PUMPKIN POTATO SOUP

Preparation time: 10 minutes   Cooking time: 20 minutes   Servings: 6

Ingredients:

4 tablespoons butter
2 pinched black pepper
1 medium carrot, roughly chopped
1 medium onion, roughly sliced
1 medium potato, roughly diced
1 cup diced pumpkin

3 tablespoons tomato paste
4 tablespoons pumpkin puree
2oz. sun dried tomatoes
1 teaspoon allspice
4 cups water
2 teaspoons salt

Directions:

In an Instant pot, combine butter, pepper, diced pumpkin, onions, and Select Saute, and cook until onions are softened. Add the potatoes, tomato paste, pumpkin puree, sun dried tomatoes, water, and salt.
Lock the lid and select Manual mode. Set the timer to 8 minutes.
When the timer beeps, turn off the pot and do a quick pressure release. Blend the contents of the Instant pot to a smooth consistency.
Serve hot with a swirl of fresh or sour cream.

CHICKEN MUSHROOM SOUP

Preparation time: 5 minutes   Cooking time: 10 minutes   Servings: 6

Ingredients:

1 tablespoon olive oil
8 oz. chicken tights, skinless, boneless, cut into chunks
2 tablespoons butter
3 cloves garlic, minced
8 oz. cremini mushrooms, sliced
1 brown onion, diced
3 carrots, peeled and diced
2 stalks celery, diced

½ teaspoon dried thyme
¼ cup all-purpose flour
4 cups chicken stock
1 bay leaf
½ cup half and half, or more, as needed
2 tablespoons chopped fresh parsley
1 sprig rosemary
Salt and pepper, to taste

Directions:

Heat olive oil in the instant pot. Select Sauté button and add chicken with salt and
Pepper. Cook for 2-3 minutes. Remove and place aside.
Add the butter, onions, mushrooms, garlic, carrot, thyme, and celery. Saute for 4 minutes.
Add flour and cook until smell like popcorns. Add the chicken stock, bay leaf and
chicken thighs. Lock the lid and select pressure cooking. Cook on high pressure for 2-3 minutes. Do a quick pressure release and stir in half and a half, season with salt and pepper and reheat the soup.
Garnish with rosemary and parsley and serve.

Broccoli Corn Chowder

Time: 20 minutes | Cooking time: 20 minutes
Preparation time: 5 minutes | Servings: 6

Ingredients:

6 ears of corn
1 cup Idaho potatoes
2 celery stalks, leaves on
1 cup broccoli florets
2 tablespoons butter
½ cup chopped brown onion

3 cups water
2 tablespoons dried parsley
2 tablespoons cornstarch
1 cup heavy cream
¼ teaspoon cayenne pepper
Salt and freshly ground pepper

Directions:

Separate the corn kernels and keep them aside.

Sauté onion and celery in butter until tender. You will do this in the Instant pot.

Add 3 cups water, cayenne pepper, parsley, and potatoes to the Instant pot. Lock the lid.

Push the manual mode button and set the timer for 8 minutes.

When the timer beeps, turn off the pot and do a quick pressure release.

Leave the corn broth in the pot and place a steamer basket. Add broccoli, corn kernels and cook for 4 minutes on high pressure. Carefully remove the steamer basket and stir the corn and broccoli into the chowder. Dissolve the cornstarch in some water and stir into the chowder.

Select Simmer and simmer the chowder until it thickens. Stir in heavy cream and season to taste. Serve after.

Red Kidney Beans soup

Preparation time: 5 minutes | Cooking time: 8 minutes | Servings: 4 minutes

Ingredients:

2 cups red kidney beans
1 tablespoon olive oil
1 brown onion, chopped
3 cloves garlic, minced
2 teaspoons cumin
1 ½ teaspoons smoked paprika
1 teaspoon salt

2 carrots, sliced
2 celery stalks, sliced
1 lb. Yukon gold potatoes
1 bunch rainbow chard
Water, to cover
Salt and pepper to taste

Directions:

Select the sauté mode and place oil in the pot. Add the garlic, onion, spices, carrots, celery, and potatoes. Cook for 3-5 minutes. Add the remaining ingredients and water to cover.

Lock the lid and select Pressure. Bring to high pressure and cook for 3 minutes.

Use quick release method to release the pressure and unlock the lid safely.

Add in the chard and place aside for 5 minutes.

Serve after.

Split Pea Ham Soup

Preparation time: 5 minutes   Cooking time: 20 minutes   Servings: 6

Ingredients:

1 lb. dried split peas
8 cups water
1 lb. ham chunks
2 brown onions, chopped

2 carrots, chopped
2 celery ribs, chopped
1 ½ teaspoons dried thyme
Salt and pepper, to taste

Directions:

Combine all the ingredients in the instant pot. Make sure that the pot is not more than half full. Lock the lid and select Pressure option.
Bring to high pressure and cook for 20 minutes.
Release pressure naturally. Check the consistency and season with salt or additional spices.
Serve hot.

Cheesy Bacon Soup

Preparation time: 5 minutes   Cooking time: 10 minutes   Servings: 6

Ingredients:

2 tablespoons butter
1 brown onion, chopped
4 cups peeled and cubed potatoes
2 (14 oz.) cans chicken broth
1 teaspoon salt
½ teaspoon pepper
¼ teaspoon red paprika flakes
2 tablespoons dried parsley

2 tablespoons cornstarch
2 tablespoons water
3 oz. cream cheese
1 cup Cheddar cheese, shredded
2 cups half-and-half
1 cup frozen corn
6 slices bacon, cooked, crumbled

Directions:

Melt butter in the Instant pot. Add onion, chopped and cook for 5 minutes.
Add 1 can chicken broth, salt, paprika flakes, dried parsley, and pepper to the onions.
Place the potatoes in the steamer basket and into the instant pot.
Lock the lid, select high pressure and cook for 4 minutes.
When the timer beeps, turn off the pressure and wait for 5 minutes to perform quick pressure release.
Carefully remove steamed potatoes from the Instant pot.
Dissolve cornstarch in water. Stir the starch into the instant pot, and simmer until thickened.
Add cheeses and cook until melted. Add remaining chicken broth, half and a half, corn, crumbled bacon, and potatoes. Heat through and serve after.

TOMATO SOUP

Preparation time: 5 minutes   Cooking time: 10 minutes   Servings: 6

Ingredients:

4 tablespoons butter
2 pinches pepper
1 large carrot, chopped
1 medium onion roughly sliced
1 medium potato, roughly diced

1 (28 oz.) canned tomato with juices
3 tablespoons tomato paste
3 tablespoons sun-dried tomatoes, chopped
4 cups water
2 teaspoons salt

Directions:

Melt the butter in instant pot. Add the onions, carrots, and cook for 5-6 minutes.
Add the canned tomatoes, potatoes, tomato paste, sun-dried tomatoes, water and salt. Lock the lid and select Pressure. Turn heat to high pressure and cook for 5 minutes. When the time is up, do a natural pressure release method. If the pressure has not come down, wait for another 10 minutes. Use the immersion blender and puree the soup. Serve while still hot.

CAULIFLOWER BACON SOUP

Preparation time: 5 minutes   Cooking time: 20 minutes   Servings: 4

Ingredients:

2 tablespoons butter
4 cups chicken stock
1 large onion, chopped
8-12 slices bacon, cooked, crumbled

4 medium potatoes
3 cups cauliflower florets
½ cup heavy cream
Salt and pepper, to taste

Directions:

Melt the butter in instant pot. Add the onions and cook until tender. Add browned bacon, potatoes, and cauliflower florets along with the chicken stock. Lock the lid and select Pressure. Cook on high pressure for 15 minutes, then do a quick release and uncover the lid. Puree the soup using an immersion blender. Stir in the heavy cream and season to taste. Serve after.

CREAMY BROCCOLI SOUP

Preparation time: 5 minutes   Cooking time: 10 minutes   Servings: 6

Ingredients:

2 cups broccoli florets
1 yellow onion
3 garlic cloves
1 tablespoon chopped celery leaves
4 tablespoons butter

1 ½ teaspoons salt
2 teaspoons black pepper
½ cup heavy cream
1 cup full-fat milk
1 ½ cups vegetable stock

Directions:

Melt the butter in instant pot. Add the onions, garlic, broccoli, and celery leaves. Cook for 3-4 minutes. Pour in the stock, and season with salt and pepper. Lock the lid and select Pressure. Cook on high pressure for 3-4 minutes. When the time is up, do a quick pressure release. Stir in the cream and milk. Puree the soup with immersion blender and reheat. Serve after.

TOMATO PUMPKIN SOUP

Preparation time: 5 minutes   Cooking time: 10 minutes   Servings: 6

Ingredients:

4 tablespoons butter
2 pinches black pepper
1 carrot, chopped
1 brown onion, roughly sliced
1 potato, roughly diced
1 (28 oz.) canned tomatoes with juices

3 tablespoons tomato paste
4 tablespoons pumpkin puree
3 tablespoons sun-dried tomatoes, chopped
1 teaspoon pumpkin spice powder
4 cups water
2 teaspoon salt

Directions:

Melt the butter in instant pot. Cook the onions and carrots for 4-5 minutes.
Place in the remaining ingredients and give it a good stir. Lock the lid and select pressure.
Bring the pressure to high and cook for 5 minutes. Use a natural pressure release. If the pressure has not come down, wait for another 10 minutes.
Blend the contents of the instant pot to a smooth consistency.
Serve while still hot.

FRESH SPINACH SOUP

Preparation time: 5 minutes   Cooking time: 10 minutes   Servings: 6

Ingredients:

4 tablespoons butter
2 pinches red peppers
3 garlic cloves, minced
1 yellow onion, chopped
50oz. spinach
1 tablespoon tomato paste

1 tablespoon sun-dried tomatoes, to garnish
1 cup heavy cream
½ cup sour fresh cream
4 cups water
2 teaspoons salt

Directions:

Heat the butter in instant pot. Cook the onions and garlic for 4-5 minutes. Add the spinach and tomato paste. Stir and add water and seasonings. Lock the lid and select Pressure. Cook on high pressure for 5 minutes. Do a natural pressure release and open the lid. Puree the spinach with an immersion blender and stir in the remaining ingredients. Reheat the soup and serve with toasted bread. Garnish with chopped sun dried tomatoes.

Sour Red beans soup

Preparation time: 5 minutes   Cooking time: 10 minutes   Servings: 6

Ingredients:

4 tablespoons butter
1 carrot, chopped
1 large red onion, roughly sliced
4 garlic cloves, minced
1 small sweet potato, roughly diced
1 (28 oz.) can red beans, rinsed

3 tablespoons tomato paste
¼ cup sour cream
2 tablespoon fresh cream
4 cups water
Salt and pepper, to taste

Directions:

Melt the butter in instant pot. Add the onions, carrots, and garlic. Cook for 4-5 minutes.
Stir in the beans, sweet potato, tomato paste, water, salt, and pepper. Lock the lid.
Select the Pressure and cook on high pressure for 5 minutes.
Use a natural pressure release.
Blend the soup with immersion blender.
Reheat the soup with heavy cream and serve in a bowl. Top with sour cream and some nachos before serving.

Chestnut soup

Preparation time: 5 minutes   Cooking time: 20 minutes   Servings: 6

Ingredients:

4 tablespoons butter
1lb. jar chestnuts, drained, rinsed
1 yellow onion, chopped
1 sprig sage
1 stalk celery, chopped
1 bay leaf

¼ teaspoon white pepper
1 potato, peeled, cubed
4 cups chicken stock
2 tablespoons rum
1 pinch nutmeg
Fresh cream, to serve with

Directions:

Heat the butter in instant pot. Add onions, carrot, celery, and sage and cook for 5 minutes.
Add potato, bay leaf, chestnuts, and chicken stock. Season with salt and pepper.
Lock the lid and select Pressure. Cook on high pressure for 15 minutes.
Do a natural pressure release. Remove a bay leaf, add the rum and nutmeg.
Puree the soup with immersion blender.
Serve with fresh cream.

ℬABY CORN CHOWDER

Preparation time: 5 minutes   Cooking time: 15 minutes   Servings: 6

Ingredients:

6 ears fresh baby corn
4 tablespoons butter
1 large yellow onion, chopped
3 cups vegetable stock
2 medium potatoes
2 tablespoons dried parsley

2 tablespoons corn starch
3 cups half and half
½ teaspoon cayenne pepper powder
4 slices bacon, cooked and crumbled
Salt, to taste

Directions:

Separate the corn kernels and keep them aside.

Heat the butter in instant pot and cook the onion until tender. Add vegetable stock, potato, and corn kernels. Stir and add parsley. Lock the lid and select Pressure. Cook on high pressure for 10 minutes. Use a natural pressure release. Dissolve starch in water and stir into the soup. Simmer until soup is thickened.

Stir in the half and half and adjust seasonings.

Ladle soup into bowls and sprinkle with crumbled bacon.

𝒢REEK SPINACH SOUP

Preparation time: 5 minutes   Cooking time: 10 minutes   Servings: 6

Ingredients:

4 tablespoons butter
2 pinches pepper
3 garlic cloves, minced
1 medium onion, roughly sliced
50oz. spinach
1 tablespoon tomato paste

1 cup heavy cream
½ cup crème Fraiche cream
½ cup feta cheese crumbled
4 cups water
Salt and pepper, to taste
Mint or basil, to garnish

Directions:

Melt butter in instant pot. Cook onions and garlic in butter until tender.

Toss in the spinach, and tomato paste. Add water and lock the lid.

Select Pressure mode and cook on high pressure for 5 minutes. Let the pressure release down naturally.

Stir in heavy cream and simmer for 5 minutes. Puree the soup using an immersion blender. Stir in crème Fraiche and serve soup in a bowl.

Top with feta cheese and some fresh basil or mint.

*S*HRIMP CORN SOUP

Preparation time: 5 minutes   Cooking time: 15 minutes   Servings: 4

Ingredients:

2 tablespoons butter
1 cup shrimps, cooked
2 medium leeks, use white and light green parts only, chopped
2 medium garlic cloves, chopped
6 corn with cobs

2 bay leaves
4 sprigs tarragon
1-quart chicken or seafood stock
Salt and pepper, to taste
1 tablespoons chives, snipped
Olive oil, to serve with

Directions:

Melt butter in Instant pot. Add sliced garlic and finely chopped leeks.

Cook till soft and tender but not browned. Now add corn with cobs, bay leaves, tarragon, and chicken or seafood stock till the corn cobs are covered. Season to taste. Seal the instant pot and cook on high pressure for 15 minutes.

Release pressure using a quick-release method and discard the cobs, tarragon, and bay leaf. Blend until smooth and strain the soup through a fine mesh.

Serve soup and top with cooked shrimps, chives, and finish off with some olive oil.

*B*EEF SOUP WITH NOODLES

Preparation time: 5 minutes   Cooking time: 15 minutes   Servings: 6

Ingredients:

1 ½ lb. lean beef, cubed
6 oz. egg noodles, cooked and drained
1/2 Spanish onion
1 28oz. can tomatoes, with juices
10 oz. baby carrots

2 teaspoon Worcestershire sauce
16 oz. chicken broth
16 oz. beef broth
1 tablespoon olive oil
Salt and pepper to season

Directions:

Select the Sauté setting on the instant pot. Heat olive oil in the pot and cook beef until browned. Place the meat aside.

Cook the onions until tender. Add remaining ingredients and give it a good stir. Place the meat back in the pot, and lock the lid. Set the High pressure and cook for 10 minutes.

After the time runs up, do a natural pressure release and add cooked egg noodles.

Simmer soup for 3-4 minutes and serve while still hot.

Leftover Chicken corn soup

Preparation time: 5 minutes   Cooking time: 20 minutes   Servings: 4

Ingredients:

2 tablespoons unsalted butter
1 cup cooked and shredded chicken, use leftovers
2 medium leeks, finely chopped
2 medium garlic cloves, sliced
6 corn with cobs, cut into halves

2 bay leaves
4 sprigs tarragon
1-quart chicken stock
Salt and pepper, to taste
Olive oil, to garnish

Directions:

Melt butter in the pot. Cook leeks, and garlic on Saute option.

Add corn with cobs, bay leaves, tarragon, and chicken stock.

Seal the Instant pot and cook on high pressure for 15 minutes.

Release pressure using a quick-release method and remove the lid.

Discard corn cobs, bay leaf, and tarragon. Blend soup using an immersion blender.

Strain the soup through a fine mesh and stir in the chicken.

Reheat the soup and serve in a bowl. Finish off with a drizzle of olive oil.

Mussel creamy soup

Preparation time: 5 minutes   Cooking time: 10 minutes   Servings: 4

Ingredients:

2 tablespoons unsalted butter
1 cup mussels, cooked
2 medium leeks, chopped, white and light green parts only
2 garlic cloves, chopped

2 cups corn kernels
2 bay leaves
4 sprigs Tarragon
1-quart chicken stock
Salt and pepper, to taste

Directions:

Melt butter in instant pot. Select Saute and cook leeks and garlic until tender.

Add corn, tarragon, bay leaf, and chicken stock.

Lock the lid and cook on high pressure for 5 minutes.

Release pressure using a quick-release pressure method and remove the lid.

Blend the ingredients using an immersion blender. Season with salt and pepper and stir in the mussels.

Reheat the soup and serve after with toasted bread.

Vegetable Noodle Soup

Preparation time: 5 minutes　　　Cooking time: 15 minutes　　　Servings: 4

Ingredients:

2 cups diced vegetables, by your choice
(carrots, parsnip, broccoli)
6 oz. noodles, cooked and drained
1 red onion, chopped
4 garlic cloves, minced
1-inch ginger, peeled, minced
2 tablespoons dried parsley

2 teaspoons dried basil
14oz. can crushed tomatoes, with juices
10 oz. baby carrots
2 teaspoons hot sauce
28 oz. vegetable stock
1 tablespoon cooking oil
Salt and pepper, to taste

Directions:

Select the Sauté setting and heat the olive oil.

Cook the onion, garlic, and ginger until fragrant. Add the veggies, and cook for 2 minutes.

Add the canned tomatoes, herbs, vegetable stock, and hot sauce.

Lock the lid and cook on high pressure for 10 minutes. Do a natural pressure release and add cooked noodles. Reheat the soup and serve after.

Chinese Noodle Soup

Preparation tie: 5 minutes　　　Cooking time: 15 minutes　　　Servings: 4

Ingredients:

2 cups diced vegetables (peppers, Shiitake
mushrooms, Asian beans, broccoli etc.)
6 oz. noodles, cooked and drained
2 green onions, chopped
4 garlic cloves, chopped
1-inch ginger, peeled, minced
1 tablespoon coconut amino

1 teaspoon white chili vinegar
10 oz. baby carrots
2 teaspoons chili sauce
28 oz. vegetable stock
1 tablespoon olive oil
Salt and pepper, to taste

Directions:

Select the Sauté setting. Heat olive oil and cook garlic, ginger, onion, and carrots.

Add coconut amino, chili sauce, chili vinegar, and vegetable stock. Cover the lid and cook on high pressure for 10 minutes.

Do a natural pressure release and add cooked noodles. Season the soup to taste and serve.

Chestnut Bacon Soup

Preparation time: 5 minutes
Cooking time:
Servings: 6

Ingredients:

4 tablespoons unsalted butter
4 to 5 bacon strips, cooked and crumbled
1lb. jar chestnuts, drained, rinsed
1 onion, chopped
1 sprig sage
1 stalk celery, chopped

1 bay leaf
½ teaspoon white pepper, ground
1 Yukon gold potato, peeled, cubed
4 cups chicken stock
2 pinches nutmeg
Salt, to taste

Directions:

Melt butter in instant pot. Cook onion, celery, sage, and white pepper until soft.

Add potato, bay leaf, chestnuts and stock.

Lock the lid and bring the pressure to high. Reduce the pressure after and cook for 15 minutes.

Do a natural pressure release and open the lid. Remove bay leaf.

Blend the soup with an immersion blender and stir in the nutmeg. Season with salt to taste, and reheat soup. Serve after, sprinkled with bacon.

SEAFOOD VEGETABLE STOCK

Preparation time: 5 minutes   Cooking time: 20 minutes   Servings: 6

Ingredients:

3 lb. mixed seafood (prawns, clams, fish etc.)
½ lb. chopped carrots
½ lb. chopped celery

½ lb. onion, chopped
1 tablespoon salt
½ teaspoon black peppercorns
Water, as desired

Directions:

Mix all the Ingredients in the Instant pot. Add enough water so the ingredients are completely covered. Cook on high pressure for 20 minutes.

Do a natural pressure release and strain stock. Flake the fish and serve with prepared stock.

PORK STOCK

Preparation time: 5 minutes   Cooking time: 20 minutes   Servings: 4

Ingredients:

3 lb. pork chopped
½ lb. chopped Spanish onions
½ lb. chopped carrots
½ lb. chopped celery

1 tablespoon Himalayan salt
½ teaspoon black peppercorns
Water, as needed

Directions:

Mix all the Ingredients in the Instant pot along with water. Add enough water to cover all the ingredients. Cook on high pressure for 20 minutes. Do a natural pressure release and strain stock. Shred the pork and serve with stock.

CLASSIC ITALIAN SOUP WITH BARLEY

Preparation time: 5 minutes   Cooking time: 15 minutes   Servings: 4

Ingredients:

1 tablespoon olive oil
2 boneless chicken breasts
3 garlic cloves, minced
1 cup onion, chopped
1 cup diced tomatoes
16 oz. spinach

15 oz. chickpeas, drained
1 cup lentils
½ cup pearl barley
3 cups chicken broth
½ cup chopped coriander
Salt and pepper, to taste

Directions:

Heat olive oil in instant pot. Select Saute and cook onions and garlic for 5 minutes.

Add barley and cook for a 1 minute.

Add remaining ingredients and give it a good stir.

Lock the lid and cook on high pressure for 10 minutes.

Do a natural pressure release and remove the chicken. Shred the chicken into pieces and place back in the pot. Simmer soup to reheat and serve after.

CHICKEN BARLEY SOUP

Preparation time: 5 minutes   Cooking time: 20 minutes   Servings: 4

Ingredients:

2 lb. skinless and boneless chicken breasts
½ cup all-purpose flour
2 garlic cloves, chopped
1 onion, chopped
1 large celery stalk, chopped
2 small carrots, chopped
2 tablespoons olive oil

1 cup sliced mushroom
14 oz. chicken broth
1/3 cup pearl barley
1 teaspoon dried oregano
½ cup red wine
Salt and pepper, to taste

Directions:

Place the flour, salt, and pepper in a bag. Add chicken and shake to coat.

Heat olive oil in instant pot. Add the chicken and cook until golden. Remove and place aside. Chop when cooled.

Cook the garlic, onion, carrot, and celery until tender.

Add the remaining ingredients and lock the lid. Cook on high pressure for 15 minutes.

Do a natural pressure release and add chopped chicken pieces. Simmer soup until reheated.

Serve hot immediately.

LEMONY CHICKEN SOUP

Preparation time: 5 minutes   Cooking time: 20 minutes   Servings: 6

Ingredients:

2 lb. boneless chicken breasts
2 teaspoon minced garlic
½ cup sliced white onion
½ cup chopped celery
½ cup chopped carrots
2 tablespoon olive oil

28 oz. can chicken broth
1/3 cup long grain rice
1 teaspoon chicken bouillon granules
Salt and pepper, to taste
2 tablespoon all-purpose flour
1/4 cup freshly squeezed lemon juice.

Directions:

Heat olive oil in instant pot and cook the chicken breast till crispy and nicely browned. Cut into fine slices.
In the same oil, sauté garlic, onions, carrots, and celery until soft. Toss in the chicken.
Add the remaining ingredients, except the all-purpose flour and lemon juice. Whisk them separately in a bowl.
Lock the instant pot lid and cook on high pressure for 10 minutes.
Do a natural pressure release and stir in the flour-lemon mixture.
Cook uncovered until the soup becomes thick.
Season with salt and pepper and serve after.

BEETROOT SOUP

Preparation time: 5 minutes   Cooking time: 20 minutes   Servings: 4

Ingredients:

1 ½ lb. beets, peeled and sliced
2 teaspoon minced garlic
½ cup sliced onion
½ cup chopped celery
1 cup chopped carrot

2 tablespoon olive oil
16 oz. can vegetable broth
3 tablespoon chopped fresh coriander
2 tablespoons crème Fraiche
Salt and pepper, to taste

Directions:

Heat olive oil in instant pot and sauté garlic, onions, carrots, and celery until tender.
Add the remaining ingredients, except the crème Fraiche.
Lock the Instant pot lid and cook on high pressure for 15 minutes.
Do a natural pressure release, and puree the soup if needed. Serve soup while still hot and top with crème Fraiche.

CORIANDER LEMON SOUP

Preparation time: 5 minutes   Cooking time: 20 minutes   Servings: 4

Ingredients:

2 teaspoon minced garlic
2 red onions, sliced
2 celery stalks, sliced
½ cup chopped carrots
2 tablespoon olive oil

16 oz. can vegetable broth
1/3 cup chopped fresh coriander
2 tablespoon all-purpose flour
¼ cup freshly squeezed lemon juice

Directions:

Heat olive oil in instant pot and sauté garlic, carrots, onions and celery until soft. Add the remaining ingredients, except the flour and lemon juice. Whisk them separately in a small bowl. Lock the Instant pot and cook on high pressure for 10 minutes. Do a natural pressure release and add the flour lemon juice mixture. Cook uncovered until the soup becomes thick. Season to taste and serve.

BEETROOT PASTA SOUP

Preparation time: 5 minutes   Cooking time: 15 minutes   Servings: 4

Ingredients:

1 cup elbow pasta, cooked
1 ½ lb. beets, peeled and diced
2 teaspoon minced garlic
2 Spanish onions, sliced
2 carrots, chopped

2 tablespoon olive oil
16 oz. can vegetable broth
4 tablespoon chopped fresh parsley
¼ cup crème Fraiche
Salt and pepper to season

Directions:

Heat olive oil in instant pot and sauté garlic, onions, and carrots until soft. Add the remaining ingredients, except the cooked pasta and crème Fraiche. Lock the lid and cook on high pressure for 15 minutes. Do a natural pressure release, strain the soup, season to taste, and stir in the pasta. Reheat soup and serve with a dollop of crème Fraiche.

SHRIMP CHEDDAR SOUP

Preparation time: 5 minutes   Cooking time: 20 minutes   Servings: 4

Ingredients:

½ cup cooked shrimps
2 teaspoon minced garlic
2 celery stalks, chopped
2 carrots, chopped
1 white onion, finely chopped
2 tablespoons olive oil

2 tablespoon cheddar cheese, shredded
16 oz. can coconut milk
¼ cup chopped fresh coriander
2 tablespoon all-purpose flour
¼ cup freshly squeezed lemon juice
Salt and pepper to season

Directions:

Heat olive oil in the instant pot. Cook garlic, carrots, onions, and celery until soft, for 5 minutes.

Add the remaining ingredients, except the shrimps, flour, and lemon juice. Whisk the flour and juice in a separate bowl.

Lock the Instant pot lid and cook on high pressure for 10 minutes.

Do a natural pressure release and add the flour mixture.

Add the cooked shrimp and cook uncovered until the soup becomes thick.

Adjust seasoning with salt and pepper.

Sharp Spinach soup

Preparation time: 5 minutes   Cooking time: 20 minutes   Servings: 4

Ingredients:

2 garlic cloves, minced
½ cup sliced onion
½ cup chopped celery
½ cup chopped carrot
2 tablespoon olive oil
1 cup spinach leaves

16 oz. can coconut milk
½ cup sharp cheddar cheese, grated
¼ cup chopped fresh coriander
Salt and pepper, to taste
2 tablespoon all-purpose flour
¼ cup beef stock

Directions:

Heat olive oil in instant pot and sauté garlic, onions and celery until tender.

Add the remaining ingredients, except the cheese, flour, and stock. Whisk the flour and stock in a separate bowl. Lock the lid and cook on high pressure for 10 minutes.

Perform a natural pressure release and stir in the cheese and flour mixture.

Cook uncovered until the soup is thick. Season before serving.

Pineapple Beets soup

Preparation time: 5 minutes   Cooking time: 20 minutes   Servings: 4

Ingredients:

1lb. beets, peeled, sliced
1 small onion, chopped
½ cup chopped celery
½ cup chopped carrot
2 tablespoon olive oil

16 oz. can vegetable broth
3 tablespoon chopped fresh parsley
Salt and pepper to season
2 tablespoon fresh coconut cream
½ cup canned pineapples, diced

Directions:

Heat olive oil in instant pot and cook onions, carrots, and celery until tender.

Add the remaining except the coconut cream.

Lock the Instant pot lid and cook on high pressure for 15 minutes.

Perform a natural pressure release. Strain the soup and top with coconut cream.

POTATO COCONUT SOUP

Preparation time: 5 minutes   Cooking time: 20 minutes   Servings: 4

Ingredients:

1 ½ lb. Yukon gold potatoes, peeled and diced
4 garlic cloves, minced
1 Spanish onion, finely chopped
½ cup chopped carrots
3 tablespoon olive oil

16 oz. can vegetable broth
2 tablespoons fresh basil, chopped
Salt and pepper to season
2 tablespoon crème Fraiche
2 tablespoon shredded cheddar cheese

Directions:

Heat olive oil in instant pot and cook garlic, onion, and carrots until tender. Add the remaining ingredients, except crème Fraiche. Lock the lid and cook on high pressure for 15 minutes.
Puree the soup with an immersion blender. Serve with a dollop of crème Fraiche and some fresh basil.

LEMON BASIL SOUP

Preparation time: 5 minutes   Cooking time: 20 minutes   Servings: 4

Ingredients:

2 tablespoons olive oil
2 garlic cloves, minced
4 medium potatoes, peeled, cubed
1/2 cup sliced onion
1/2 cup chopped carrot

16 oz. can vegetable broth
½ cup chopped fresh basil leaves
2 tablespoon all-purpose flour
1/4 cup freshly squeezed lemon juice
Lemon pepper, to taste

Directions:

Heat olive oil in instant pot and cook garlic, onion, and carrots until tender. Add the remaining ingredients except for flour and lemon juice. Whisk them separately in a bowl. Lock the lid and cook on high pressure for 10 minutes. Perform a natural pressure release and whisk in the lemon-flour mixture. Cook uncovered until the soup is thick. Serve in a bowl and sprinkle with lemon pepper.

CHICKEN BARLEY SOUP

Preparation time: 5 minutes   Cooking time: 20 minutes   Servings: 4

Ingredients:

2 lb. boneless and skinless chicken breasts, sliced
½ cup all-purpose flour
1 onion, chopped
1 chopped celery
1 chopped carrot
2 tablespoon olive oil

1 cup oyster mushrooms
14 oz. chicken broth
½ cup pearl barley
1 teaspoon dried oregano
½ cup white wine
Salt and pepper, to taste

Directions:

Combine the flour, salt, and pepper in a bag. Add the chicken slices and shake to coat evenly.
Heat the oil in the instant pot and cook the chicken until golden. Place aside and shred when cooled.
Remove the chicken and cook the onions, garlic, celery, and carrots for 5 minutes.
Add the remaining ingredients in the pot and lock the lid. Cook on high pressure for 15 minutes.
Perform a natural pressure release and add shredded chicken pieces. Simmer the soup briefly and serve after.

ASIAN STYLE SOUP

Preparation time: 5 minutes   Cooking time: 20 minutes   Servings: 4

Ingredients:

2 cups diced vegetables, by your choice
3 oz. fried rice noodles, to garnish
2 white onions, chopped
4 cloves garlic minced
½- inch ginger, minced
1 cup oyster mushrooms
1 teaspoon soy sauce

1 teaspoon white chili vinegar
10 oz. baby carrots
2 teaspoon chili sauce
28 oz. vegetable stock
1 tablespoon sesame seeds oil
Salt and pepper to season
Roasted crushed peanuts, to garnish

Directions:

Select the Sauté on instant pot. Add the sesame oil and cook the onions, garlic, ginger until fragrant. Add the remaining veggies and mushrooms. stir to coat. Add the soy sauce, chili sauce, chili vinegar, and vegetable stock. Cover the lid and cook on high pressure for 10 minutes. Perform a natural pressure release method. Ladle soup into bowls, and top with fried noodles and crushed peanuts.

MEXICAN SOUP

Preparation time: 5 minutes   Cooking time: 25 minutes   Servings: 6

Ingredients:

4 tablespoons butter
1 large carrot, chopped
1 medium onion, roughly sliced
4 garlic cloves, minced
1 (28 oz.) can black beans, rinsed, drained
4 tablespoons tomato paste

1 cup shredded Mexican cheese
½ cup half-and-half or fresh cream
1 handful coriander, chopped
4 cups beef stock
Salt and pepper, to taste
Crushed tortilla chips, to garnish

Directions:

In an Instant pot, melt butter. Cook the garlic, onions, and carrot. Add the canned black beans, tomato paste, and stock. Season to taste with salt and pepper. Lock the lid and cook on high pressure for 5 minutes.
When the time is up, perform a natural pressure release method.
Stir in the remaining ingredients, coriander, cheese, and a half and half.
Simmer soup for 5 minutes and serve garnished with crushed tortilla chips.

TOFU SOUP

Preparation time: 5 minutes   Cooking time: 15 minutes   Servings: 4

Ingredients:

2 tablespoon unsalted butter
½ cup diced firm tofu
2 medium leeks, chopped, white and light green parts only
2 medium garlic cloves, sliced thinly
1 cup corn kernels

2 bay leaves
2 sprigs tarragon
4 cups chicken stock
Salt and pepper, to taste
1 tablespoon chives, snipped
Extra-virgin olive oil, to garnish

Directions:

Melt butter in the instant Pot. Add sliced garlic and finely chopped leeks.
Cook until tender. Add all the remaining Ingredients, except the chives.
Lock the lid, select pressure mode and cook on high pressure for 10 minutes.
Discard bay leaf and tarragon. Puree the soup with an immersion blender and ladle soup into bowls.
Sprinkle with snipped chives before serving.

PUMPKIN SOUP

Preparation time: 10 minutes   Cooking time: 12 minutes   Servings: 6

Ingredients:

3 cups cubed pumpkin
3 cups vegetable broth
1 coconut milk
1 onion, diced
3 garlic cloves, chopped

1 pinch sea salt
1 teaspoon black pepper
1 teaspoon ginger powder
2 tablespoons olive oil

Directions:

Set Instant pot to saute. Add the olive oil, garlic, onion, and pumpkin.
Place in the rest of the remaining ingredients. Give them a good stir.
Set to manual and cook for 10 minutes.
Allow the pressure to release on its own before opening.
Serve while still hot.

CLASSIC VEGETABLE SOUP

Preparation time: 10 minutes   Cooking time: 12 minutes   Servings: 4

Ingredients:

2 large potatoes, diced
1 yellow onion, diced

2 cloves garlic, chopped
1 teaspoon black pepper

1 carrot, diced
1 cup diced celery

½ cup diced fennel
3 cups vegetable broth

Directions:

Set Instant pot to saute. Add in the olive oil, garlic, onion, celery, and potatoes. Cook for 5 minutes.
Add in the rest of the remaining ingredients and stir.
Set to manual and cook for 10 minutes.
Allow the pressure to release on its own. Serve while still hot.

POTATO SOUP

Preparation time: 10 minutes   Cooking time: 12 minutes   Servings. 6

Ingredients:

2 tablespoons olive oil
3 cups cubed red potatoes
1 brown onion, diced
2 cloves garlic, chopped

2 teaspoon black pepper
2 carrots, diced
4 cups vegetable broth
2 tablespoons dried parsley

Directions:

Set Instant pot to saute. Add in the olive oil, garlic, onion, carrots, and potatoes. Cook for 5 minutes.
Place in the rest of the ingredients and lock the lid.
Set to manual and cook for 10 minutes.
Allow the pressure to release naturally.
Serve while still hot with homemade bread.

CORN FISH SOUP

Preparation time: 10 minutes   Cooking time: 6-8 hours

Ingredients:

2 onions, sliced into rings
1lb. white fish without bones, any kind
2 cups corn
3 cloves garlic, chopped
2cups vegetable broth

2 cups coconut milk
½ cup coconut cream
1 teaspoon black pepper
2 teaspoons onion powder

Directions:

Place the Ingredients in the Instant pot.
Cook on the slow cook setting for 6-8 hours.
Serve with toasted bread.

TOMATO CELERY SOUP

Preparation time: 10 minutes   Cooking time: 3-4 hours   Servings: 4

Ingredients:

2 onions, sliced
2 cups tomato sauce
1 handful fresh basil
1 cup sundried tomatoes, chopped

4 cloves garlic, chopped
2 cups vegetable broth
1 teaspoon black pepper
1 teaspoon celery flakes

Directions:

Place all ingredients the Instant pot. Stir and lock the lid.
Cook on the slow cook setting for 3-4 hours. Serve while still hot.

SPICY CARROT SOUP

Preparation time: 10 minutes   Cooking time: 6-8 hours   Servings: 6

Ingredients:

3 cups carrots, shredded
½ cup ginger, peeled and chopped
3 cups vegetable broth

1 teaspoon black pepper
1 teaspoon garlic powder

Directions:

Place the Ingredients in instant pot. Stir well and cook on the slow cook setting for 6-8 hours.
Use an immersion blender to puree the soup. Serve while still hot with toasted bread slices.

THAI SOUP

Preparation time: 10 minutes   Cooking time: 6-8 hours   Servings: 6

Ingredients:

2large potatoes, chopped
1 cup chicken breasts, cut into bite-sized pieces
1cyellow onion, chopped
1 tablespoon cornstarch
1 cup celery, chopped
1 carrot, chopped
3 cloves garlic, chopped
5 cups chicken broth

2 cups coconut milk
1 cup coconut cream
2 tablespoons Curcuma
2 tablespoons chili powder
2 tablespoons lemongrass
1 teaspoon onion powder
1 teaspoon black pepper
2 teaspoons garlic powder

Directions:

Place all the ingredients in the Instant pot. Lock the lid. Cook on the slow cook setting for 6-8 hours.
Serve with toasted bread slices.

SPLIT PEA SOUP

Preparation time: 10 minutes   Cooking time: 6-8 hours   Servings: 6

Ingredients:

3 large red potatoes, chopped
1 ½ cups dried peas
2 cups ham, cut into bite-sized pieces
1 Spanish onion, chopped

2 carrots, chopped
5 cups chicken broth
1 teaspoon black pepper
1 teaspoon garlic powder

Directions:

Place the Ingredients in the instant pot. Stir well and lock the lid. Cook on the slow cook setting for 6-8 hours. Serve with bread slices.

CREAMY CELERY SOUP

Preparation time: 10 minutes   Cooking time: 6-8 hours   Servings: 6

Ingredients:

2 celery roots, sliced
3 cups celery stalks, chopped
1 onion, chopped
2 carrots, chopped
4 cloves garlic, chopped

6 cups vegetable broth
2 teaspoons onion powder
1 teaspoon black pepper
1 tablespoon dried parsley
1 cup cream cheese, softened

Directions:

Place all the ingredients in instant pot. Stir and lock the lid.
Cook on the slow cook setting for 6-8 hours.
Serve with bread slices and garnish with grated cheddar cheese.

DILL POTATO SOUP

Preparation time: 10 minutes   Cooking time: 6-8 hours   Servings: 6

Ingredients:

5 red potatoes, diced
½ cup fresh dill weed, chopped
2 celery stalks, chopped, chopped
1 brown onion, chopped onion, chopped
1 cup cream cheese

¼ cup heavy cream
2 cloves garlic, chopped
6 cups vegetable broth
1 teaspoon onion powder

Directions:

Place the ingredients in instant pot. Stir and lock the lid.
Cook on the slow cook setting for 6-8 hours.
Serve with warm bread.

$\mathcal{P}$UMPKIN RICE SOUP

Preparation time: 10 minutes   Cooking time: 6-8 hours   Servings: 6

Ingredients:

1 cup long-grain rice
2 cups cauliflower florets
1 onion, chopped
2 cups pumpkin, cubed
2 carrots, grated

2cloves garlic, chopped
5 cups chicken broth
1 cup coconut milk
1 tablespoon coconut oil
Salt and pepper, to taste

Directions:

Heat the oil in instant pot. Add the onion, garlic, and carrots. Cook for 5 minutes. Add the remaining ingredients and give it a good stir.
Lock the lid and cook on the slow cook setting for 6-8 hours.
Serve while still hot.

$\mathcal{Q}$UINOA BEEF SOUP

Prep time: 10 minutes   Cooking time: 6-8 hours   Servings: 6

Ingredients:

1 cup quinoa, rinsed
1 cup broccoli florets
1 cup beef steak strips
1 yellow onion, chopped
1cup black beans, soaked overnight, rinsed
2 carrots, chopped

2ccloves garlic, chopped
5 cups vegetable broth
1 cup coconut milk
1 tablespoon dried parsley
Salt and pepper, to taste

Directions:

Place the Ingredients in the Instant pot. Stir and lock the lid.
Cook on the slow cook setting for 6-8 hours.
Serve with bread slices.

$\mathcal{C}$HICKEN CHILI SOUP

Preparation time: 10 minutes   Cooking time: 6-8 hours   Servings: 4-6

Ingredients:

4 cup chicken broth
2 cups black beans, soaked overnight, rinsed
1 cup chopped tomatoes
2 tablespoons tomato paste

1 teaspoon chili powder
1 teaspoon garlic powder
½ cup shredded chicken
2 tablespoons sour cream
1 cup shredded cheddar cheese

Salt and pepper, to taste

Directions:

Combine all ingredients in instant pot, except the sour cream.
Lock the lid and cook on low setting for 6 hours.
Serve with a dollop of sour cream.

BEEF STEW

Preparation time: 10 minutes   Cooking time: 6-8 hours   Servings: 6

Ingredients:

2 large potatoes, chopped
1 cup beef stew meat, cut into bite-size pieces
1 yellow onion, chopped
1 tablespoon cornstarch (mixed with water)
1 cup celery, chopped

1 carrot, chopped
2 cloves garlic, chopped
5 cups beef broth
1 teaspoon black pepper
1 tablespoon dried parsley
3 tablespoons tomato paste

Directions:

Combine all ingredients, except the starch in an instant pot. Stir and lock the lid.
Cook on low setting for 6-8 hours.
Use a natural pressure release and open the lid. Stir in the cornstarch mixture and simmer until it is thick.
Serve after.

INDIAN STYLE STEW

Preparation time: 10 minutes   Cooking time: 6-8 hours   Servings: 6

Ingredients:

3large potatoes, chopped
2 cups chicken, cut into bite-sized pieces
1 yellow onion, chopped
1 tablespoon cornstarch (whisked with water)
1 cup frozen spinach, thawed
2 carrots, chopped

4 cloves garlic, chopped
5 cups chicken broth
2 cups coconut milk
1 cup coconut cream
1 teaspoon Curcuma
2 tablespoons chili powder
Salt and pepper, to taste

Directions:

Combine all ingredients, except the starch in an instant pot. Stir and lock the lid.
Cook on low setting for 6-8 hours.
Use a natural pressure release and open the lid. Stir in the cornstarch mixture and simmer until it is thick.
Serve after.

CLAM CHOWDER

Preparation time: 10 minutes   Cooking time: 6-8 hours   Servings:

Ingredients:

4 small gold potatoes, peeled, cubed
2 cups clams, cleaned
1 cup clam juice
3 cups vegetable stock
4 cups heavy cream
1 scallion, chopped
1 tablespoon cornstarch

1 carrot, chopped
2 cloves garlic, chopped
1 cup chicken broth
1 teaspoon black pepper
1 cup bacon, chopped
2 teaspoons onion powder
1 teaspoon ginger powder

Directions:

Combine all ingredients, except the starch in an instant pot. Stir and lock the lid.

Cook on low setting for 6-8 hours.

Use a natural pressure release and open the lid. Stir in the cornstarch mixture and simmer until it is thick. Serve after.

SAUSAGE SOUP

Preparation time: 10 minutes   Cooking time: 6-8 hours   Servings: 6

Ingredients:

1 sweet potato, peeled, cubed
3 cups spicy sausage, sliced into bite-sized pieces
2 scallions, chopped
1 tablespoon cornstarch (mixed with water)
1 cup black beans, soaked overnight

1 carrot, chopped
2 cloves garlic, chopped
5 cups chicken broth
1 tablespoon chili powder
Salt and pepper, to taste

Directions:

Combine all ingredients, except the starch in an instant pot. Stir and lock the lid.

Cook on low setting for 6-8 hours.

Use a natural pressure release and open the lid. Stir in the cornstarch mixture and simmer until it is thick. Serve after.

Main courses

MAC AND CHEESE

Preparation time: 5 minutes Cooking time: 5 minutes Servings: 4

Ingredients:

8 oz. macaroni
¾ cup half-and-half
½ teaspoon dried mustard
4 oz. Monterey Jack grated cheese
4 oz. shredded cheddar cheese

2 cups warm water
½ teaspoon salt
¾ cup milk
Pinch of cayenne pepper
Fresh ground black pepper – to taste

Directions:

Combine macaroni, water, mustard, salt and cayenne pepper in an instant pot.
Lock the lid and select low pressure.
Once the pressure reaches the right pressure, set a cooking timer to 4 minutes.
Perform a quick pressure release when 5 minutes are up.
Remove lid and stir in half-and-half and milk; select "brown" option on the instant pot and cook for 1-3 minutes, until thickens, stirring often.
Add cheese, gradually stirring until melted.
Season with pepper and serve while still hot.

WHITE CHICKEN CHILI

Preparation time: 5 minutes Cooking time: 20 minutes Servings: 6

Ingredients:

3 cups cooked chicken
1 onion, sliced
2 tablespoons cornmeal
2 jalapeno peppers, sliced
2 can green chilies, chopped
4 garlic cloves, minced
1 lb. great northern beans, rinsed
8 cups chicken stock

1 ½ tablespoons ground cumin
½ teaspoon paprika
½ teaspoon cayenne pepper
Salt – to taste
2 tablespoons butter
Some olive oil
½ cup half-and-half

Directions:

Chop all ingredients and prepare instant pot.
Place green chilies, jalapeno peppers, onion, and garlic in an instant pot; add some olive oil and butter.
Press start button on instant pot just to heat for browning.
Cook vegetables for 5 minutes; turn off the instant pot.

Add white beans chicken stock; stir well. Close and lock the lid; a program to 15 minutes.

Release pressure naturally and remove the lid. Let it cool for 5-10 minutes.

Stir in spices, chicken and add water if too thick; stir well.

Press the start button just to bring the mix to a simmer.

Combine cornmeal and half-and-half until smooth; stir in chili.

Simmer for 10 minutes and turn off the instant pot, by pressing the cancel button. Serve while still hot.

*I*NSTANT POT FISH

Preparation time: 5 minutes   Cooking time: 5 minutes   Servings: 4

Ingredients:

4 white fish fillets
4 spring onions, sliced into rounds
1 cup white wine or fish stock
Juice from 1 orange

Zest from 1 orange
1-inch piece ginger, chopped
Some olive oil
Fresh ground salt and pepper – to taste

Directions:

Rinse fish and pat dry with kitchen towels.

Rub olive oil into fish and season with salt and pepper.

Combine white wine, ginger, spring onions, orange juice, and zest into the instant pot.

Place fish fillets into a steamer basket and lock the lid.

Bring the instant pot to medium pressure and cook for 3 minutes.

Release pressure naturally and carefully open the lid.

Serve fish while still warm with ginger-orange sauce.

*T*ERIYAKI CHICKEN WINGS

Preparation time: 5 minutes   Cooking time: 15 minutes   Servings: 4

Ingredients:

2 lb. chicken wings
2 tablespoons sugar
6 tablespoons sesame oil
½ teaspoon crushed red pepper

1 cup low sodium teriyaki sauce
1 tablespoon lemon juice
Some toasted sesame seeds – to garnish

Directions:

Combine sugar, 4 tablespoons sesame seeds oil, teriyaki sauce, crushed red pepper and lemon juice in a bowl.

Add chicken wings and cover with plastic foil; refrigerate for 2-3 hours.

Heat remaining sesame oil in instant pot over high heat; when starts to sizzle add drained chicken wings.

Reserve marinade. Brown chicken wings for couple minutes, all sides.

Pour over the reserved marinade and cover with lid; cook on high for 7 minutes.

Let the pressure release naturally for 10 minutes and perform quick release to safely remove the lid.

Serve while still hot, garnished with sesame seeds.

*I*NSTANT PORK RIBS

Preparation time: 5 minutes   Cooking time: 25 minutes   Servings: 4

Ingredients:

2 lb. boneless country-style pork ribs, cut
into 2-inch pieces
1 teaspoon pepper
1 teaspoon paprika
1 teaspoon onion salt
3 tablespoons tomato puree

1 cup water
1 teaspoon mustard
1/8 teaspoon celery seed
4 ½ teaspoon white wine vinegar
1 tablespoon vegetable oil
1 teaspoon Worchester sauce

Directions:

Sprinkle the ribs with pepper, paprika and onion salt.

Heat vegetable oil in instant pot over medium.

Add ribs and brown on all sides.

Remove from the instant pot and drain; return to the instant pot.

Combine remaining ingredients water, wine vinegar, Worchester sauce, celery seeds and tomato puree in a bowl. Pour over meat and close the instant pot; bring the cooker to full pressure.

Reduce heat to medium and cook for 15 minutes.

Remove from the heat and allow pressure to drop on its own.

Serve while still hot.

*C*HICKEN ADOBO

Preparation time: 5 minutes   Cooking time: 5 minutes   Servings: 4

Ingredients:

1 whole chicken, cut in parts, skinned or 2
lb. chicken tights, bone in
2 bay leaves
1 cup water
1 cup low sodium soy sauce

1 tablespoon finely chopped garlic
1 green onion, sliced
1 teaspoon honey
1 tablespoon finely grated ginger

Directions:

Combine all ingredients in instant pot, except honey.

Bring to boil and secure with lid.

Bring to high pressure and cook for 8 minutes.

Turn off the heat and let the pressure release naturally for 10 minutes; perform quick release to safely remove the lid.

Pull the meat off the bones and set in a bowl; combine remaining honey with sauce in an instant pot and pour over meat in a bowl.

Serve with rice or veggies.

INSTANT MAPLE GLAZED HAM

Preparation time: 5 minutes   Cooking time: 25 minutes   Servings: 6

Ingredients:

1 bone-in ham
½ cup honey
½ cup maple syrup

2 tablespoons orange juice
1 teaspoon nutmeg
1 teaspoon cinnamon

Directions:

Combine all ingredients, except ham, in a saucepan over medium-high heat and mix ingredients well.
Place the ham in an instant pot and cook for 15 minutes over medium pressure, lid closed.
Release pressure on its own and transfer ham into oven safe dish preheat broiler.
Baste generously ham with honey-maple mix and set under the broiler to get a nice crust.
Slice before serving.

KINGS CRAB

Preparation time: 5 minutes   Cooking time: 5 minutes   Servings: 4

Ingredients:

4lb. king crab legs
4 tablespoons melted butter
1 cup water or vegetable stock or fish stock

4 lemon wedges
Some chopped dill

Directions:

Before you start with the cooking you should break the crab legs so they fit in an instant pot.
Add the water or stock and chopped dill.
Lock the lid and select the fish option on the instant pot. Bring to medium pressure and maintain the pressure for 3 minutes.
Use a quick pressure release and remove the crab legs.
Drizzle with melted butter and serve with lemon wedges.

GLAZED TURKEY

Preparation time: 5 minutes   Cooking time: 35 minutes   Servings: 16

Ingredients:

10lb. turkey, whole
6oz. apricot jam
1 ½ cups chicken stock
1 yellow onion, diced
½ teaspoon ground cumin
½ teaspoon ground coriander seed

¼ teaspoon ground cloves
2 carrots, peeled and diced
Salt and pepper, to taste

Directions:

In a small bowl, combine the spices and apricot jam.

Pat dry rinsed turkey and brush the entire surface with prepared glaze.

Place the trivet into an instant pot. Place the carrots, onion, and stock into an instant pot.

Place the turkey on a trivet and lock the lid.

Select the meat option and bring the pressure to high. Maintain the pressure for 30 minutes. Once you hear the beep, release the pressure naturally. Remove the turkey and carve before serving. To get that crunchy skin, broil the turkey for 5 minutes.

STUFFED ONIONS

Preparation time: 5 minutes   Cooking time: 25 minutes   Servings: 6

Ingredients:

12 small onions
1 egg
5 medium potatoes
2 cups vegetable or chicken stock

¾ cup grated parmesan
3 tablespoons fresh thyme
Fresh ground salt and pepper
Some olive oil

Directions:

Prepare the potatoes: place potatoes in an instant pot and add water up to half their height and a spoon of salt. Close and lock the lid and bring to medium pressure; reduce heat to the minimum required to maintain pressure. Cook potatoes for 15 minutes.

Prepare the onions; peel and make slices at the bottom so they can stand upright. Using melon baller scoop out the middle. Mash potatoes and when cooled stir in the egg and thyme; season with salt and pepper.

Stuff the onions with prepared potato filling and place in instant pot.

Pour over chicken stock and sprinkle with grated cheese; drizzle with olive oil.

Close the lid and lock; turn the heat to high and when the cooker starts to whistle lower the heat and cook for 10-15 minutes.

Release pressure naturally and open the instant pot.

Remove onions and serve while still hot.

CHICKEN MARSALA

Preparation time: 5 minutes   Cooking time: 25 minutes   Servings: 4

Ingredients:

2 cups dry Marsala wine
4-6 chicken tights
1 cup sliced mushrooms
1 cup sliced onions
1 tablespoon dried basil
1 tablespoon dried oregano
½ tablespoon minced garlic

½ cup mascarpone cheese
1 tablespoon butter
½ cup parmesan cheese
Some parsley to garnish
Cooked pasta or rice to serve with
Fresh ground salt and pepper

Directions:

Season chicken meat with fresh ground salt and pepper.

Place mushrooms, onions, and garlic in an instant pot; press the start button and sauté ingredients for 5 minutes over melted butter.

Add basil and oregano and give it a good stir.

Press cancel to shut off the instant pot.

Pour in Marsala wine and add chicken; shut the lid and program the instant pot for 20 minutes; press start.

Meanwhile, prepare pasta according to package instructions.

After 20 minutes release pressure naturally. Remove chicken to a platter.

Add in mascarpone and stir until melts.

Place back the chicken back in the instant pot and coat chicken with sauce thoroughly.

Serve with prepared pasta and sprinkle with parmesan cheese and parsley.

CORNED BEEF AND CABBAGE

Preparation time: 5 minutes   Cooking time: 70 minutes   Servings: 6

Ingredients:

3 lb. cured corned beef
1 bottle beer
2 cups potatoes, cut into halves or chunks

2 cups carrots, chopped
1 cup onion, chopped
2 cups shredded cabbage

Directions:

Place the onion in an instant pot and add beer.

Place the corned beef with spices in an instant pot as well.

Set the lid and adjust pressure cook time button to 60 minutes.

Press start button and prepare remaining ingredients.

Slice carrots, potatoes and shred the cabbage.

Release the pressure; add potatoes and carrots. Shut the lid and program the instant pot to 10 minutes and press start.

When cycle is complete release the pressure and remove the lid; add cabbage and place the lid.

Do not heat the instant pot but just let the cabbage rest in a hot instant pot. Slice beef and serve after 6-7 minutes.

FAST BEEF STEW

Preparation time: 5 minutes   Cooking time: 25 minutes   Servings: 6-8

Ingredients:

3 lb. stewing beef, boneless, cut into 1-inch cubes
1/3 cup all-purpose flour
3 tablespoons olive oil
1 tablespoon tomato paste

1 ½ cups beef stock
2-3 fresh thyme springs
1/3 cup all-purpose flour
1 ½ cups red wine
1 cup diced onion

2 carrots, peeled and cut into ½-inch pieces
2 celery stalks, cut into ½-inch pieces
2 garlic cloves, crushed

½ lb. new potatoes, cut into ½-inch cubes
2 garlic cloves, crushed
Fresh ground salt and pepper – to taste

Directions:

Toss the beef with flour, salt, and pepper in a large bowl.

Coat evenly and transfer in heated electric pressure with olive oil; cook the beef over medium heat until browned.

If your instant pot is small, you can work in batches; transfer beef to a bowl.

Add wine to the electric pressure and bring to a simmer; deglaze the cooker by scraping down the brown bits.

Return the beef to instant pot and add the celery, potatoes, tomato paste, carrots, stock, and thyme; stir to combine.

Cover and secure the lid; cook on medium for 20 minutes.

Release the pressure according to manufacturer's instructions.

Serve while still hot.

COLOMBIAN CHICKEN STEW

Preparation time: 5 minutes   Cooking time: 25 minutes   Servings: 4

Ingredients:

4 chicken legs, cut into tights and drumsticks
1 onion, chopped
4 potatoes, peeled and cut into 1-inch chunks

4 cups diced tomatoes
2 bay leaves
Salt and pepper, to taste

Directions:

Combine all ingredients in an instant pot. Season to taste.

Gently toss with clean hands.

Lock the lid and bring to medium pressure. Maintain the pressure for 25 minutes.

Quick-release the pressure and serve while still hot.

MONGOLIAN BEEF

Preparation time: 5 minutes   Cooking time: 35 minutes   Servings: 4

Ingredients:

2lb. flank steak, cut into 1-inch wide strips
¾ cup water
2 tablespoons cornstarch
4 garlic cloves, minced
½ cup soy sauce, low-sodium
3 spring onions, sliced

1 tablespoon oil
2/3 cup brown sugar
1-inch ginger, peeled and minced
Salt and pepper, to taste

Directions:

Season the beef with salt and pepper.

Set the instant pot to brown and add the oil. Once hot, add the beef and cook until browned. Remove the beef and place aside.

Add the garlic into an instant pot and cook until fragrant. Add the soy sauce and ½ cup water.

Stir in the ginger and brown sugar. Add the beef and lock the lid. Bring to medium pressure and maintain the pressure for 15 minutes. After 15 minutes use a quick pressure release. Meanwhile, whisk the remaining water and cornstarch. Open the instant pot and stir in the cornstarch mix. Select simmer and bring to boil, stirring until sauce thickens.

Stir in the chopped spring onion and serve while still hot.

SPINACH CHICKEN STEW

Preparation time: 5 minutes   Cooking time: 55 minutes   Servings: 4

Ingredients:

1 cup baby spinach, roughly chopped
1 cup chopped yellow onion
1 cup white beans
1 cup coconut milk
1 tablespoon ghee

2 tablespoons mild curry powder
4 cups water
2 chicken breasts, boneless and skinless
Fresh ground salt and pepper

Directions:

First, cook the chicken; cut chicken breasts in half and place in instant pot. Add one cup of water and season with salt and pepper. Cover with lid tightly and cook on medium for 12 minutes. Once the chicken breasts are done, release the pressure according to manufacturer's instructions. Remove the chicken and set to plate to cool down. Discard cooking water and place cooking pot back in the electric pressure. Start the electric pressure and set to medium heat, and stovetop to low; add ghee and when melted add onion, chopped. Cook for 1-2 minutes. Add curry powder and mix to combine; turn off the electric instant pot or remove the stove pot from the stove. Add coconut milk, beans, and remaining water. Stir gently and shut the lid; program the instant pot to cook for 30 minutes or cook for 20 minutes at the stove. Meanwhile, shred the cooked chicken. When the cooking is finished remove the lid and stir in baby spinach and cooked chicken. Stir well to combine and additionally season with salt and pepper.

JUICY TURKEY BREASTS

Preparation time: 5 minutes   Cooking time: 35 minutes   Servings: 8

Ingredients:

6lb. turkey breast, skin on, bone-in
1 yellow onion, quartered
3 tablespoons water
3 tablespoons cornstarch
14oz. chicken broth

1 cup diced celery stalk
1 sprig thyme
Salt and pepper, to taste

Directions:

Season the turkey breast with salt and pepper.

Place a trivet or a rack into an instant pot. Add the onion, broth, celery, and thyme into the instant pot.

Place the turkey breast on a trivet, skin side down and lock the lid.

Bring to medium pressure and maintain the pressure for 30 minutes. Use a natural pressure release. Remove the turkey from the instant pot and skim off any fat.

Whisk the water and cornstarch and stir in the cooking broth. Select saute and stir until broth thickens. Season the sauce to taste.

Remove the skin from turkey and slice it up. Serve with prepared the sauce.

*I*NSTANT PORK CHOPS

Preparation time: 5 minutes   Cooking time: 25 minutes   Servings: 4

Ingredients:

2 cups button mushrooms, chopped
4 pork chops
1 onion, chopped
6 potatoes, peeled and chopped
6 oz. can tomato sauce

6oz. water
1 red bell pepper, chopped
4 carrots, peeled and coarsely chopped
½ tablespoon olive oil
Salt and pepper, to taste

Directions:

Heat the olive oil in an instant pot.

Brown the pork chops and remove. Drain off the excess fat.

Add the carrots, bell pepper and tomatoes into an instant pot.

Combine the water and tomato sauce and pour into the instant pot.

Place the pork chops back in the instant pot and lock the lid. Bring the pressure to medium and cook for 15 minutes.

Use a natural pressure release. Serve the chops while still hot.

*D*E LUXE MEATLOAF

Preparation time: 5 minutes   Cooking time: 30 minutes   Servings: 4

Ingredients:

1lb. ground beef
1lb. ground pork
8 bacon slices
½ cup milk
3 bread slices, crumbled

3 eggs, beaten
2 tablespoons dried parsley
1 cup grated Parmesan cheese
½ cup BBQ sauce
Salt and pepper, to taste

Directions:

In a large bowl, combine the milk and crumbled bread. Let the bread soak.

Add the pork, beef, parsley, eggs, and parmesan cheese. Season to taste and mix with clean hands.

Place the trivet into an instant pot and pour in 2 cups water. From a meatloaf and wrap with bacon slices. Brush the meatloaf with ½ BBQ sauce and place onto the trivet.

Lock the instant pot and bring to medium pressure. Maintain the pressure for 20 minutes. Once you hear the beep from the instant pot, quick release the pressure. Remove the meatloaf and brush with remaining BBQ sauce. Preheat the broil and broil the meatloaf for 5 minutes. Slice and serve.

SIMPLE PULLED PORK

Preparation time: 5 minutes   Cooking time: 60 minutes   Servings: 4

Ingredients:

4lb. pork shoulder, boneless, cut into 2 pieces
2 cups BBQ sauce
2 tablespoons olive oil

½ cup water
1 teaspoon cayenne pepper
Salt and pepper, to taste

Directions:

Select the browning option on your instant pot and add the olive oil.

Brown pork on both sides, for 3-4 minutes. Remove and place aside.

Add water, cayenne pepper, and 1 cup BBQ sauce in the instant pot.

Add the browned pork and lock the lid. Select the medium pressure and maintain the pressure for 50 minutes. Use a natural pressure release.

Remove the lid and remove the meat from the cooker. Pull the pork with two forks. Reserve ½ cup cooking liquid and place in a saucepan. Add remaining BBQ sauce and pork. Bring to a simmer. Cook for 4-5 minutes more. Serve on toasted rolls.

AMAZING LAMB SHANKS

Preparation time: 5 minutes   Cooking time: 40 minutes   Servings: 4

Ingredients:

4 lamb shanks
1 tablespoon sunflower oil
15oz. can diced tomatoes, with juices
4 garlic cloves, crushed
1 tablespoon tomato paste
1 teaspoon oregano

1 teaspoon dried chopped thyme
½ cup red wine
1 cup chicken stock
1 brown onion, diced
Salt and pepper, to taste

Directions:

Season the lamb shanks with salt and pepper.

Select the brown option and heat the oil.

Brown the lamb shanks in the instant pot. Remove and place aside.

Add the garlic, onion, and herbs. Cook for 5 minutes and add the tomato paste.

Add the tomatoes and wine. Bring the mix to a simmer and scrape down any bits. Stir in the stock.

Add the lamb shanks and any juices left in the bowl. Lock the lid and bring the pressure to medium.

Maintain the pressure for 30 minutes. Turn off the heat and release pressure naturally.
Remove the lamb from the cooker and strain the cooking juices through a sieve. Transfer the juices to a small sauce pot and cook until slightly reduced. Serve the lamb shanks with prepared sauce.

CHICKEN CHORIZO DELIGHT

Preparation time: 5 minutes   Cooking time: 15 minutes   Servings: 6

Ingredients:

3 tablespoons olive oil, extra-virgin
8 oz. sausage, sliced chorizo
3 cups onion, chopped
2 tablespoons garlic, minced
2 grams bell pepper
1 ½ lb. chicken, skinless thighs
1/2 teaspoon salt

1/2 teaspoon ground pepper
3 cups wine, white
4 cups tomatoes
2 cups water
1/4 cup parsley, flat
5 saffron threads

Directions:

Heat the oil in the instant pot on Saute function without closing the lid.
Add the sliced chorizo sausage and cook for about 5 minutes.
Add the minced garlic, chopped onion, bell pepper, tomatoes, parsley and saffron, and the chicken.
Season with salt and pepper and stir in the wine and water.
Cook for a minute before closing and locking the lid to set to Poultry mode pressure cooking. When done, release the pressure.
Transfer to a serving platter and top with a sprinkling of your favorite shredded cheese.

PORK AND GRAVY

Preparation time: 5 minutes   Cooking time: 15 minutes   Servings: 6

Ingredients:

1 ½ lb. pork roast, fatty cut
1 teaspoon kosher salt
½ teaspoon black pepper
4 cups cauliflower, chopped

1 onion, medium chopped
4 cloves garlic
4oz. celery, sliced
8 oz. mushrooms, button sliced

3 tablespoons coconut oil
2 cups water

Directions:

Arrange the cauliflower, garlic cloves, onion, and chopped celery at the bottom of your instant pot. Add 2 cups of water. Season the pork with kosher salt and ground pepper. Place the pork in the pot and cook for 50 minutes on high pressure. Release pressure naturally and open the lid. Preheat your oven to 350F. Transfer the pork into baking dish and pop in the oven for 20 minutes. Empty your instant pot by transferring the cooked veggies and broth to a blender and process until smooth in texture. Set the instant pot on SAUTE function and cook the mushrooms in oil. Add the blended veggies and continue to sauté until the blended mixture is thickened. Serve with pork.

TURKEY WITH CRANBERRIES

Preparation time: 5 minutes   Cooking time: 15 minutes   Servings: 4

Ingredients:

1 ½ lb. turkey breasts
1 teaspoon salt
1 teaspoon freshly ground pepper
3 tablespoons canola oil, divided
4 shallots, peeled and quartered
1 teaspoon dried thyme

1 cup chicken broth
For the cranberry sauce:
1 ½ cups cranberries
¼ cup dried cranberries
2 tablespoons brown sugar
1 tablespoon vinegar, apple cider

Directions:

Rub turkey breasts with half a teaspoon of salt and half a teaspoon of pepper.

Set your instant pot to SAUTE function on High pressure; set the timer to 20 minutes.

Heat half of the canola oil in the heated instant pot; add the seasoned turkey and cook until browned on all sides.

Add the remaining ingredients; press cancel and switch to poultry function; set the timer to 35 minutes.

Once done, do a Quick Release method to release steam pressure.

Open the lid and add the cranberry sauce ingredients.

Set to Manual and cook for 10 minutes.

When done, do the Natural Release method to release steam pressure.

Slice while still hot.

CHICKEN WITH PAPAYA

Preparation time: 5 minutes   Cooking time: 15 minutes   Servings: 4

Ingredients:

4 tablespoons olive oil
1 teaspoon ginger, peeled and minced

1 brown onion, sliced
1lb. chicken thighs
1 tablespoon fish sauce

4oz. papaya cut into bite-sized cubes
4oz. kale leaves

Directions:

Set your instant pot to SAUTE function and adjust the timer to 10 minutes. Add 4 tablespoons olive oil, ginger, onion, fish sauce and the chicken tights. Cook until browned.

Flip chicken thigh pieces to the other side to brown evenly.

Add 1 cup of water in your instant pot. Cover with the lid, lock and seal the valve.

Select Poultry and cook for 15 minutes.

Once done, do a quick release to let off steam. Open the lid and add the papaya and water.

Set to manual and cook on high for 10 minutes. Add the kale and cook for 5 minutes.

Serve after.

Wrapped Chicken with Sauce

Preparation time: 5 minutes | Cooking time: 15 minutes | Servings: 4-6

Ingredients:

1 lb. chicken breast
½ lb. bacon
4 tablespoon coconut oil

½ cup heavy whipping cream
3 tablespoon butter
2 tablespoon Dijon mustard

Directions:

Slice the chicken breast filet into bite- sized pieces and wrap each piece with a bacon slice.

Set the instant pot to Saute. Add the oil and brown the bacon wrapped chicken.

Lock the lid and cook on Poultry settings for 10 minutes. Open the lid and remove the chicken.

Select the Manual and melt the butter in the pot. Add the remaining ingredients and simmer until sauce is thick.

Cheesy Hot Dogs

Preparation time: 5 minutes | Cooking time: 5 minutes | Servings: 6

Ingredients:

1 lb. hot dogs
1 lb. bacon slices
2oz. cheddar cheese
1 teaspoon garlic powder

1 teaspoon onion powder
½ teaspoon salt
½ teaspoon pepper
2 cups water, to cook the hotdogs

Directions:

Set your instant pot to SAUTE function on high. Add 2 cups of water.

Score hot dogs with a slit in each lengthwise where the cheese can be stuffed.

Slice a couple of ounces of cheese into rectangular strips just about the length of your hot dogs. Insert the cheese strips in the hotdog.

Wrap around the hotdog a slice of bacon and seal with a wooden pick.

Set the wrapped hot dogs on the steamer basket. Place the steamer basket in the preheated instant pot.

Place the hot dogs on top of the steamer basket. Lock the lid and cook for 5 minutes.

Use a quick pressure release and serve after.

Chuck Roast

Preparation time: 5 minutes | Cooking time: 40 minutes | Servings: 4-6

Ingredients:

2 lb. chuck roast
½ teaspoon salt
¼ teaspoon black pepper

4 tablespoons ghee
1 onion, chopped
1 clove garlic, minced

1 tablespoon tomato paste
2 cups broth
¼ cup red wine
1 tablespoon soy sauce

1 ½ lb. Swedish turnip
1 lb. carrots
8 oz. mushrooms

Directions:

Rub the chuck roast with pepper and salt.

Put the ghee in the instant pot; set to SAUTE function.

When the ghee is heated up, add the chuck roast to brown all sides. Remove and place aside.

Add the onion and cook for 3 minutes.

Add the tomato paste and garlic; continue cooking until fragrant.

Stir in the broth, soy sauce, and red wine; return the chuck roast and simmer for 10 minutes.

Lock the lid and select Manual. Cook on high pressure for 35 minutes.

Once the time is up, do a Quick Release method to let out the steam pressure.

Open and transfer the cooked chuck roast to a baking sheet; add the carrots, Swedish turnip, and mushrooms and cover the pot. Select the MEAT function on HIGH pressure for 5 minutes.

While the veggies are cooking, broil the roast under 5 minutes or until crispy.

Do a quick-release method to let out steam and select Saute until liquid is reduced to half.

Serve with the cooked veggies.

BRAISED CHICKEN WITH WALNUTS AND ORANGE

Preparation time: 5 minutes   Cooking time: 25 minutes   Servings: 4

Ingredients:

2 tablespoons butter
2 tablespoons olive oil
1 lb. chicken legs
1 teaspoon salt
1 teaspoon pepper

1 onion, medium size, sliced
1 cup thyme, fresh
1 cup cranberries
1 cup walnuts, shelled
1 cup orange juice

Directions:

Heat you Instant pot to high in Saute function without closing the lid.

Add the olive oil and butter to melt.

Brown the chicken legs in the pot and season with salt and pepper.

Remove the chicken and add the sliced onion. Cook for 4 minutes. Place back the browned chicken legs and add the walnuts, cranberries, thyme and orange juice.

Lock the lid and select Manual. Set the timer to 20 minutes.

Release the pressure naturally.

Carefully transfer the chicken legs to a serving platter. Top with onions, cranberries, and walnuts.

Simmer the remaining liquid until reduced. Drizzle over chicken legs before serving.

$\mathcal{P}$ORK SHRIMPS PATTIES

Preparation time: 5 minutes   Cooking time: 5 minutes   Servings: 6

Ingredients:

½ lb. pork, ground
½ lb. shrimp, chopped
½ lb. daikon, grated
3oz. shiitake mushrooms, chopped
1 scallion, chopped
1 teaspoon sesame seeds
1 tablespoon corn starch

1 tablespoon almond, flour
1 teaspoon soy sauce
½ teaspoon salt
½ teaspoon pepper
½ cup beer or water
1 tablespoon olive oil

Directions:

In a medium size bowl, combine the all the ingredients except for 1 tablespoon olive oil and 1 tablespoon butter. Mix well and shape the mixture into the desired number of patties.
Set the instant pot on Saute function and pour in the beer or water and insert steam tray.
Place the patties onto steaming tray and lock the lid. Bring to high pressure and cook for 5 minutes.
Use a natural pressure release and open the lid.
If you want that crispy crust, heat the olive oil in a skillet. Fry the patties for 1 minute per side.
Serve after.

$\mathcal{S}$IMPLE SIRLOIN STEAK

Preparation time: 5 minutes   Cooking time: 20 minutes   Servings: 6

Ingredients:

2 lb. beef sirloin steak
4 tablespoons mayonnaise

2 tablespoons Dijon mustard
1lb. provolone cheese

Directions:

Place a steamer base basket and a cup or two cups of water in your instant pot.
Brush the steak pieces with mayo and mustard; arrange steak pieces in a baking tray; top each piece with a slice of provolone cheese; place the baking tray on top of the steamer basket.
Close and lock the lid and seal the valve of your instant pot.
Set the Instant pot on MEAT function at high; set the timer to 20 minutes.
Wen done, carefully release the pressure manually by swinging the valve pressure release quickly.
Open the Instant pot lid after all steam had been released.
Serve steaks after.

PORK STEAKS

Preparation time: 5 minutes   Cooking time: 15 minutes   Servings: 6

Ingredients:

2 lb. pork steak
2 tablespoons olive oil
1 tablespoon brown sugar
1 tablespoon oyster sauce
1 tablespoons ketchup or tomato puree
1 tablespoon apple cider vinegar
2 teaspoons Dijon mustard
1 teaspoon Worcestershire sauce

¼ teaspoon garlic powder
1/8 teaspoon onion, powder
1/8 teaspoon sea salt
1/8 teaspoon cayenne
1/8 teaspoon black pepper, ground
1 tablespoon Sriracha sauce
1 cup water

Directions:

Set the instant pot on SAUTE function; brown the steaks in olive oil.

Once browned, switch to a Manual.

Add the remaining ingredients and simmer for 10 minutes, before closing the lid.

Cook for 30 minutes and do a quick pressure release.

Serve with mashed potatoes.

JUICY MEATBALLS

Preparation time: 5 minutes   Cooking time: 15 minutes   Servings: 6

Ingredients:

½ lb. shrimps, chopped
1 lb. ground pork
¼ cups carrots, finely diced
1 teaspoon black pepper
¼ cup coconut, oil
2 large eggs
¼ cup green onions, chopped
1 tablespoon sea salt

2 tablespoons coconut, flour
3 cloves garlic, minced
2 yellow onions, chopped
2 cups vegetable broth
3 cups water
2 teaspoons fish sauce
1 bunch spinach

Directions:

In a large bowl, combine the shrimp and ground pork with carrots, black pepper, sea salt, coconut flour, green onions, and eggs; mix to combine well. Shape the mixture into 12 balls.

Set your instant pot to SAUTE function. Brown the meatballs and make room for the garlic, pepper, and onion to sauté for 3-4 minutes.

Add the fish sauce, water, and broth. Lock the lid and select Soup function.

When the cycle is done, perform a natural release method.

Open the lid and stir in the spinach.

Serve while still hot.

ASPARAGUS AND SMOKED BACON

Preparation time: 5 minutes   Cooking time: 5 minutes   Servings: 6

Ingredients:

2 lb. Asparagus   1lb. smoked bacon

Directions:

Pre-heat your Instant pot in STEAM function on HIGH pressure without closing the lid.

Add 1 to 2 cups of water to the inner pot.

Wrap each asparagus stick with a slice of smoked bacon.

Lay a few asparagus sticks on the steamer basket in a single layer.

Lay the smoked bacon wrapped asparagus sticks on the single layer of unwrapped asparagus sticks.

Repeat layering until all your wrapped asparagus is in the basket, are neatly arranged in the steamer basket before lowering it in the inner pot of your instant pot.

Lock the lid and set the timer to High pressure for 3 minutes.

Wien did, use the Natural Release method to open the instant pot.

Serve after.

SALMON SUSHI ROLLS

Preparation time: 10 minutes   Cooking time: 5 minutes   Servings: 4

Ingredients:

16 oz. cauliflower   ½ avocado, peeled, pitted
6 oz. cream cheese softened   5 oz. smoked salmon
1 tablespoon mirin rice vinegar   1 cup parsley, chopped
1 tablespoon soy sauce   1 pack Nori sheets
1 cucumber, seeded and sliced into strips 2 tablespoons olive oil

Directions:

Using a blender, grind cauliflower into corn meal-size crumbs.

Place the crumbled cauliflower in your instant pot. Set to Manual mode, close, lock and seal the vent; set the timer to 5 minutes.

As soon as you hear the timer beep, slide the valve open to release pressure quickly.

Take out the cauliflower rice and transfer to a bowl.

Sprinkle mirin and light soy sauce over the cauliflower rice; stir gently just to incorporate

Slice the avocado in half, scoop out the meat and slice into strips. Slice cucumber into long thin strips along with the smoked salmon.

Lay a sheet of Nori sheet wrapper on a bamboo mat or roller. Brush the nori sheet with olive oil and place a spoonful of cauliflower mixture over the nori sheet; leave an inch of open space from the top edge.

Arrange slices of avocado, cucumber and smoked salmon about one and a half inches from the bottom edge of your cauliflower mixture. Roll the sheet from the bottom edge tightly.

Slice the cauliflower rolls into bite size pieces and serve.

CHICKEN LETTUCE WRAP

Preparation time: 5 minutes   Cooking time: 25 minutes   Servings: 4

Ingredients:

1 lb. chicken breast
4 tablespoons coconut oil
3 tablespoons apple cider vinegar
1 teaspoon ground cumin

1 teaspoon ground mustard
1 teaspoon paprika
1 teaspoon black pepper
6 lettuce leaves, romaine

Directions:

In a small mixing bowl, combine the apple cider vinegar with coconut oil, cumin, mustard, paprika and black pepper; mix well. Rub the chicken breast with the vinegar, 2 tablespoons of oil and spices mixture; marinade for at least 30 minutes. Set your instant pot to SAUTE function on HIGH pressure and adjust the timer to 10 minutes. Add the remaining oil and brown the chicken breasts. Add 2 cups of water in your instant pot. Press CANCEL and shift to the Poultry function on HIGH. Set the timer to 20 minutes. When done, remove the chicken breasts from the instant pot and shred the chicken breasts when cool enough to handle. Get a piece of lettuce leaf scoop onto it about 2 tablespoons of shredded chicken; sprinkle the shredded chicken filling with leftover oil, vinegar and spices mixture before folding the lettuce leaf to the shredded chicken filling. Serve immediately.

INSTANT SQUID

Preparation time: 5 minutes   Cooking time: 15 minutes   Servings: 4

Ingredients:

2 tablespoons olive oil
2 grams anchovy
1 clove garlic, smashed
1 onion, chopped
1 teaspoon red pepper flakes
1lb. tomatoes
2 lb. squid sliced in rings

½ cup white wine
1 red bell pepper
1 tablespoon lemon juice
1/4 teaspoon salt
2 tablespoons olive oil
1 cup parsley, chopped

Directions:

Set your instant pot to SAUTE function on HIGH pressure and add 2 tablespoons of olive oil; stir in the anchovy, minced garlic, onion, and red pepper flakes.
Stir in the squid rings and lightly brown them a bit. Add the wine and let it reduce to a minimum. Add the tomatoes, half a cup of parsley and a cup of water.
Press cancel and shift to MANUAL function on HIGH pressure and set the timer to 15 minutes. Close, lock the lid and when done, release the pressure by the Quick Release method. Open the lid and stir in the juice of 1 lemon, the remaining half a cup of parsley and olive oil.
Serve after.

TUNA SPREAD WITH BACON

Preparation time: 5 minutes   Cooking time: 7 minutes   Servings: 4

Ingredients:

2 large eggs
1 can tuna flakes in olive oil
1 tablespoon chopped onion
4oz. bacon, cooked and crumbled
2 teaspoons whole grain mustard

¼ teaspoon dried dill
1 tablespoon mayonnaise
1 tablespoon sour cream
Iceberg lettuce

Directions:

Place a steamer base basket and a cup or two cups of water in instant pot. Place the eggs on top of the steamer basket. Close and lock the lid and seal the valve of your instant pot.

On STEAM function, set the timer to 7 minutes. Once done, use quick pressure release method.

Open the instant pot lid after all steam had been released and transfer the eggs to an ice-cold water. Peel the eggs after 15 minutes and chop finely.

Add the tuna flakes, chopped onion, crumbled bacon, prepared mustard, dill, mayonnaise and sour cream. Toss well and serve on iceberg lettuce or bread slices.

TACO FRITTATA

Preparation time: 5 minutes   Cooking time: 15 minutes   Servings: 4

Ingredients:

1 lb. ground beef
1 tablespoon taco seasoning
¾ cup water
6 large eggs
1 cup heavy whipping cream

2 cloves garlic, minced
½ teaspoon salt
¼ teaspoon pepper
1 cup shredded Cheddar cheese

Directions:

Set the instant pot on SAUTE function; grease a 6-inch baking dish with butter.

Without the lid on, brown the ground beef for 8 to 10 minutes inside the instant pot.

Add the taco seasoning and stir well to incorporate.

Add half a cup of water and continue cooking until sauce thickens.

Once done transfer the beef taco mixture to a greased 6-inch baking dish.

Wash the inner pot of your pressure cooker; return the pot and fill in 2 cups water.

Combine eggs, heavy whipping cream, garlic, salt and pepper In a large bowl; mix well and pour over beef taco mixture; sprinkle top with shredded cheddar cheese.

Set the instant pot on STEAM function on HIGH pressure and set the timer to 15 minutes.

Place your steamer basket and the baking dish with your beef taco egg mixture.

When done, use a natural pressure release method.

Serve tacos with avocado slices.

LIME BRAISED PORK CHOPS

Preparation time: 5 minutes   Cooking time: 25 minutes   Servings: 6

Ingredients:

½ teaspoon ground cumin
2 tablespoons garlic, minced
1 teaspoon black pepper
1 teaspoon salt

2 lb. pork chop, sirloin
1/2 cup tomato sauce
1 lime, juiced
3 tablespoons butter

Directions:

In a small mixing bowl, combine the spices with salt; rub this mixture over the pork chops.
In a separate mixing bowl, combine the tomato sauce with the lime juice.
Set your instant pot in SAUTE function. Add the butter and brown the pork chops.
Add the tomato-lime mixture to cover the browned pork chops.
Close, lock, and seal the vent valve; press CANCEL and shift to HIGH pressure.
Cook for 20 minutes.
Serve after.

BURGUNDY STEW

Preparation time: 5 minutes   Cooking time: 15 minutes   Servings: 4

Ingredients:

1 lb. beef flank steak
2 tablespoons coconut oil
2 cloves garlic, minced
2 teaspoon rock salt
2 tablespoons thyme
2 tablespoons parsley
2 teaspoon ground black pepper

½ lb. bacon
1 onion, sliced
½ cup carrots, julienned
1 cup red wine
1 tablespoon maple syrup
½ cup beef broth

Directions:

Set your instant pot to Saute function; add the coconut oil.
In a small bowl, combine salt and spices and rub this mixture on beef.
Cut the bacon into strips and brown the strips in instant pot.
Add the seasoned beef steaks, and the remaining ingredients.
Lock the lid and shift to MEAT function on HIGH pressure.
Adjust the timer to desired cooking duration.
Release pressure naturally and serve while still hot.

OXTAIL STEW

Preparation time: 5 minutes   Cooking time: 35 minutes   Servings: 6

Ingredients:

2 ½ lb. beef oxtail
6 cloves garlic, minced
½ lb. string beans
1 yellow onion, sliced
1 teaspoon turmeric

1 medium eggplant, cut into chunks
1 tablespoons fish sauce
½ lb. Napa cabbage
6 tablespoons peanut butter
3 tablespoons shrimp paste

Directions:

Put your instant pot in SAUTE function and brown the oxtail. Add the garlic and onion; sauté for about 5 minutes.

Place all the remaining ingredients , except the Napa cabbage leaves and shrimp paste, in your instant pot.

Lock the lid and select the Meat function on HIGH pressure. Set the timer to 30 minutes.

Use a quick pressure release method and open the lid. Add the cabbage and shrimp paste.

Select Manual and simmer for 5 minutes.

Serve after.

BEANS BEEF CASSEROLE

Preparation time: 5 minutes   Cooking time: 20 minutes   Servings: 4

Ingredients:

2 tablespoon olive oil
2 lb. ground beef
½ cup onion, chopped
1 teaspoon salt
1 teaspoon dried parsley

1 teaspoon black pepper, ground
1 teaspoon oregano
½ cup cheddar cheese
2 cups green beans
4 mozzarella sticks

Directions:

On Saute function in your instant pot, brown the ground beef in olive oil.

Add the chopped onion, herbs, spices, and salt.

Remove the browned beef from the pot.

Clean the instant pot and fill with 2 cups water; place the trivet inside the pot.

Arrange the beans, browned beef, cheddar cheese, and mozzarella.

Cover and lock the instant pot's lid. Set to Steamer function and adjust the timer to 15 minutes.

When done, use a quick pressure release.

Carefully remove the baking dish and serve the casserole while still hot.

Hungarian Meatballs

Preparation time: 5 minutes   Cooking time: 15 minutes   Servings: 4

Ingredients:

1 lb. Hungarian sausage, casing removed
1 large egg
¼ teaspoon salt
1 cup almond flour

8 oz. cheddar cheese
2oz. grated parmesan
1 tablespoon butter
2 teaspoon baking powder

Directions:

Set your instant pot in Steam function. In a bowl, combine the eggs and spices and beat well.

Add remaining ingredients and shape the mixture into meatballs.

Put the sausage balls on a greased baking dish that can fit inside your instant pot.

Cover, lock and seal the vent valve and set the timer to 15 minutes.

Serve while still hot with favorite sauce.

Chicken Vegetable Salad

Preparation time: 10 minutes   Cooking time: 8 minutes   Servings: 6

Ingredients:

3 lb. chicken breast
4oz. roasted peppers
1 cup celery, chopped
½ cup sliced basil
½ cup scallion, chopped

½ cup olive oil
½ cup vinegar, white wine
1 tablespoon mustard
5oz. arugula

Directions:

Set your instant pot on Poultry function. Add the chicken breasts and a cup of water.

Close and lock the lid of your instant pot and cook for 8 minutes. Release pressure naturally.

Take out the cooked chicken breasts from your instant pot and shred.

Place shredded chicken breasts in a medium size bowl; add the chopped peppers, basil, celery, and scallions.

In a small bowl, mix together the olive oil, mustard, and vinegar and pour the mixture over the bowl of shredded chicken and veggies. Toss to combine.

Arrange a bed of arugula on your serving platter topped with your shredded chicken veggie salad and serve.

Chuck Eye Stew

Preparation time: 5 minutes   Cooking time: 35 minutes   Servings: 6

Ingredients:

3 tablespoons olive oil
2 lb. beef, chuck eye roast

1 onion, sliced
2 teaspoons garlic, minced

4 teaspoons rosemary , chopped
1 teaspoons thyme, chopped
2 tablespoons soy sauce
8 tablespoons butter
4oz. sweet potatoes

½ cup broccoli, florets chopped
½ cup carrots, chopped
3 tablespoons tomato paste
¼ cup coconut milk

Directions:

On Saute function brown the beef in olive oil; add the onions and garlic followed by rosemary, thyme, and soy sauce; add a cup of water.

Cover, lock and seal the valve; press cancel and shift to the MEAT function and cook for 20 minutes.

Do the quick release method when done; open the pot and add the butter, sweet potato, broccoli and carrots. Reset the timer and cook for additional 15 minutes. Do a quick pressure release.

Open the lid and pour in the tomato paste and coconut milk. Lock the lid again, set to Manual and cook for 5 minutes. For the last time use a quick pressure release and serve stew while still hot.

COD IN CREAMY SAUCE

Preparation time: 5 minutes   Cooking time: 25 minutes   Servings: 4

Ingredients:

1 lb. mushrooms
3 oz. butter
1 teaspoon salt
1 teaspoon ginger, minced
2 tablespoons parsley
2 cups heavy cream

3 tablespoons Dijon mustard
½ lb. shredded cheese
1 ½ lb. cod
1 ½ lb. cauliflowers florets
3 oz. olive oil

Directions:

Set the instant pot to Saute function and add the butter.

Slice the mushrooms and cook in butter; season with the herbs, salt, and pepper.

Stir in the mustard and heavy whipping cream; switch to LOW mode. Simmer uncovered for about 5-10 minutes to infuse sauce reduction. Season cod fish with pepper and salt; carefully arrange the pieces in the pot. Add the broccoli as well. Sprinkle the cheese over fish and broccoli.

Cover, lock the lid and seal the vent valve. The shift to Manual function and set the timer to 15 minutes.

When done, do the Quick Release method to release steam pressure. Serve after.

BACON AND SPINACH

Preparation time: 5 minutes   Cooking time: 10 minutes   Servings: 4

Ingredients:

5 oz. bacon sliced to bite size pieces
½ lb. spinach leaves
3 eggs, large
1 cup heavy cream

5 oz. cheese, shredded
2 tablespoons butter
Salt and pepper, to taste

Directions:

Preheat your instant pot on Steam function.

Place the steamer basket in the inner pot and pour 2 cups of water.

Place a baking dish on top of the steamer basket.

Add the butter and bacon to baking dish and top with spinach.

Mix the eggs and cream in a medium-size mixing bowl; transfer the mixture to the baking dish with bacon and spinach.

Sprinkle shredded cheese on top of the mixture.

Lock the lid of the instant pot and seal the vent.

Set the timer to 10 minutes.

Do a Quick Release when done and serve while still hot.

BEANS WITH TOMATOES AND CHICKEN

Preparation time: 5 minutes   Cooking time: 10 minutes   Servings: 4

Ingredients:

3 tablespoons olive oil
¾ lb. chicken breasts, sliced into strips
1 garlic clove, minced
1 cup tomatoes, chopped
½ cup onion, sliced

½ teaspoon salt
½ teaspoon black pepper, ground
4oz. green beans
1 teaspoon dried basil

Directions:

Set the instant pot on SAUTE function. Add the oil and brown the chicken strips.

When done, push the browned strips to one side of the pan and add the garlic, tomatoes, and onions. Cook for 2 minutes. Lock the lid and shift to Manual. Set the timer for 5 minutes.

When done, do a natural pressure release.

Serve while still hot.

MANGO WITH SALMON

Preparation time: 5 minutes   Cooking time: 17 minutes   Servings: 4

Ingredients:

¼ cup coconut oil
1lb. grams salmon fillet strips, with skin on
1 teaspoon salt
1 teaspoon fish sauce
¼ cup vinegar, coconut
2 tablespoons ginger, crushed

½ cup tomatoes, sliced
½ cup onion, sliced
1 teaspoon black pepper, coarsely ground
5 cups water
2oz. green mango powder (Amchoor)
5oz. mustard leaves

Directions:

Place all the ingredients in the instant pot, except the mustard leaves.

Lock the lid and press the Soup function. Cook for 15 minutes.

Once done, do the Quick pressure release method.

Open the lid and add the mustard leaves; press cancel and shift to MANUAL function; adjust the timer to 2 minutes. Serve after.

STEAMED LEMONY SALMON PACKETS

Preparation time: 10 minutes   Cooking time: 10 minutes   Servings: 4

Ingredients:

1 tablespoon olive oil
1 ½ lb. salmon fillet
1 tablespoon honey
1 teaspoon salt
1 teaspoon pepper

1 onion, sliced in rings
1 lemon, sliced
1 teaspoon dried thyme leaves
4 parsley sprigs

Directions:

Take 4 large pieces of parchment paper.

Coat your salmon fillets with olive oil, honey, salt and pepper

Lay the parchment paper on your work table and begin layering your ingredients - 1 salmon fillet, onion rings and a slice of lemon.

Fold up the paper packet. Cut a piece of aluminum foil enough to wrap your paper packet.

Pour a couple of cups of water in your instant pot.

Put your steamer basket inside the instant pot. Arrange two salmon fillets packets in a steamer basket.

Lock the instant pot lid. Set the pressure to high on Steam function; when the instant pot reaches the right pressure, turn down the heat to the lowest pressure maintenance level.

Cook for ten 10 minutes. Release the pressure naturally when done.

Remove the packets from the instant pot. Gently remove the aluminum foil and set the fillet packets on individual plates. Tear the parchment paper just before serving.

TACO BEEF

Preparation time: 5 minutes   Cooking time: 15 minutes   Servings: 6

Ingredients:

2 lb. beef, ground
2 tablespoons olive oil
2 tablespoons chili powder
2 teaspoons ground cumin
2 teaspoons sea salt
1 teaspoon paprika.
½ teaspoon onion powder
½ teaspoon garlic powder
½ teaspoon dried oregano

½ teaspoon crushed red pepper
For the cheese sauce:
6 tablespoons butter
6 tablespoons coconut, flour
2 cups whipping cream
2 cups cheddar cheese
1 cup almond milk
16 oz. mozzarella

Directions:

On SAUTE function of your instant pot, brown the ground beef in olive oil; add the remaining ingredients and transfer to a low tempered glass baking dish.

Combine all the ingredients of the cheese sauce in a small mixing bowl; pour over the browned beef in the baking dish; place the baking dish in a steamer basket; wash the inner pot of the instant pot and put 2 cups of water; place the trivet inside the inner pot with water.

Place the baking dish with the taco beef mixture on top of the steamer basket.

Cover and lock the instant pot's lid. Press cancel and switch to Meat function on high. Set the timer to 25 minutes. When done, release the pressure by doing the quick pressure release method.

Serve while still hot.

GINGER STEAMED SALMON

Preparation time: 5 minutes   Cooking time: 15 minutes   Servings: 6

Ingredients:

- 1 teaspoon garlic, minced
- 2 teaspoons ginger, crushed
- 1 teaspoon fish sauce
- 1 teaspoon lemon, juice
- 2 lb. salmon, filet
- 1 cup sour cream
- 1 tablespoon mayonnaise
- ½ teaspoon, dill weed
- ¼ teaspoon, garlic powder
- ¼ teaspoon, onion powder

Directions:

In a small bowl, combine the garlic, ginger, fish sauce, and lemon juice. Rub the mixture over all sides of the salmon filets.

Apply non-stick cooking spray to your steamer basket and place it inside your instant pot filled with 2 cups of water.

Place the salmon filet over the steamer basket, skin side down; set the instant pot on Steam function on HIGH pressure and set the timer to 20 minutes. Meanwhile, combine the remaining ingredients to create a dill-mayonnaise dip. Chill the dip in the fridge.

When done, perform a quick pressure release.

In a small bowl, combine the ingredients for your dipping sauce and serve with steamed salmon filets.

BEEF WITH BROCCOLI AND MUSHROOMS

Preparation time: 5 minutes   Cooking time: 15 minutes   Servings: 4

Ingredients:

- 1 ½ lb. ground beef
- ½ cup red wine
- 5oz. sliced mushrooms
- 5oz. broccoli, cut into florets
- 3oz. spinach, raw
- 2 tablespoons coconut amino
- 2 teaspoons garlic, minced
- 2 teaspoons minced ginger
- 1 tablespoon five spice
- 1 tablespoon pepper
- 1 teaspoon salt
- 2 teaspoons cumin

1 teaspoon cayenne pepper
½ teaspoon onion powder

3 tablespoons ketchup

Directions:

Brown ground beef in instant pot on high heat at Saute setting. Add the minced garlic and ginger. Sauté the beef mixture for about 6 minutes or until the beef is browned.

Stir in the broccoli with the coconut amino and all the spices.

Stir in the red wine and add the mushrooms. Lower the heat and continue to sauté for another 10 minutes.

Add the spinach and continue to sauté for 4 minutes.

Remove from heat; transfer to a plate and serve with ketchup.

SMOKED BRISKET

Preparation time: 5 minutes   Cooking time: 15 minutes   Servings: 4

Ingredients:

1lb. beef brisket
2 tablespoons brown sugar
2 teaspoons salt
1 teaspoon black pepper
1 teaspoon mustard powder

1 teaspoon onion, powder
½ teaspoon smoked paprika
2 cups beef broth
2 thyme sprigs
3 tablespoons coconut oil

Directions:

In a small mixing bowl, combine the brown sugar with spices. Rub the beef brisket with the prepared blend.

Set your instant pot to SAUTÉ; add coconut oil. Brown the beef brisket on all sides.

Add the remaining ingredients and cover the pot, lock the lid and seal the vent valve.

Select Manual and set the timer to 50 minutes.

When done, perform a natural pressure release method to let out steam pressure.

Take out the cooked meat and cover with aluminum foil.

Press CANCEL and switch to SAUTE function once more; set the timer to 10 minutes.

With the lid off, simmer the liquid until reduced.

Serve with brisket.

TUNA ADOBO

Preparation time: 5 minutes   Cooking time: 15 minutes   Servings: 4

Ingredients:

¼ cup olive oil
1lb. tuna belly
1 teaspoon salt
¼ cup coconut amino
¼ cup coconut vinegar
2 teaspoons garlic, crushed
1 tablespoon ginger, minced

1 teaspoon black pepper, coarsely ground
¼ cup butter, melted
7oz. spinach

Directions:

On Steam function on the High pressure of your instant pot, set the timer to 15 minutes; pour 2 cups of water into the inner pot of the cooker.

Take a shallow baking tin pan, add the oil and lay the tuna belly slab skin side down over the baking pan. Place the pan with tuna belly on your steamer basket. Combine the coconut amino, vinegar, salt, pepper and crushed garlic in a small mixing bowl. Pour the prepared mixture over tuna belly.

Insert the steamer basket with the pan in your instant pot.

When done do a quick pressure release method.

Open the lid and add the butter and spinach; close the lid without closing the valve, press cancel and shift to Manual function and set the timer to 1 minute.

Once done, serve immediately.

TUNA AND PECANS

Preparation time: 5 minutes   Cooking time: 15 minutes   Servings: 6

Ingredients:

2 lb. tuna
½ cup pecan nuts, crushed
½ cup mayonnaise
½ cup grapes, seedless sliced in halves

Salt and pepper to taste
Dash of ginger powder
Iceberg lettuce, to serve with

Directions:

Cut tuna into bite size cubes and season with salt, pepper and ginger powder.

Place the tuna cubes in a heat tempered baking dish and cover the dish with aluminum foil.

Place the dish over the trivet in the inner pot of your instant pot filled with 2 cups of water.

Close the lid, lock and seal the valve. Press the Steam button on high pressure and set the timer to 15 minutes.

Release the pressure when done with the natural release method.

Transfer the cooked tuna cubes to a mixing bowl and toss in all the remaining ingredients.

Serve on a bed of iceberg lettuce.

THREE CHEESE EGGPLANT STACK

Preparation time: 5 minutes   Cooking time: 15 minutes   Servings: 4

Ingredients:

8oz. spinach, fresh leaves
1 ¼ cups feta cheese
1 cup mozzarella cheese, grated
4oz. Parmesan cheese grated
6 eggs, large

3oz. ghee
½ tsp salt
1 teaspoon chopped fresh oregano
1 teaspoon chopped fresh basil
1 cup marinara sauce

Directions:

Pour 2 cups water in instant pot.

Preheat the instant pot on STEAM function on High.

Slice the eggplants in ½-inch thick slices. Grease the tempered baking dish with ghee. Arrange the eggplants in the baking dish and season with salt and pepper.

Place the dish in the instant pot. Close and lock the lid and set the timer to cook for 10 minutes. Do a quick release method when done.

Remove the eggplants and place aside.

Blanch the spinach by boiling water and dipping the spinach in it for at least 58 seconds. Transfer blanched spinach leaves to a bowl of cold water and drain excess water after 5 minutes.

Beat the eggs in a small bowl and cook on a stove top with your fry pan to do some thin omelet spread.

Assemble lasagna; place 2 omelets at the bottom of a baking pan.

Spread some Marinara sauce over the omelets. Do the layers alternately using a layer of all the ingredients - eggplant slices, mozzarella cheese, spinach, and half of the crumbled feta cheese.

Place the baking dish in the instant pot and lock the lid. Set to Steam function and cook for 15 minutes.

Use the Quick release method when done and serve while still hot.

MARINATED WHOLE CHICKEN

Preparation Time: 60 minutes   Cooking Time: 40 minutes   Servings: 6

Ingredients:

1 whole chicken, skinless	½ teaspoon chili powder	½ teaspoon cumin powder
1 cup yogurt	1 tablespoon black pepper	2 tablespoon soya sauce
2 tablespoon lemon juice	1 teaspoon salt	4-5 tablespoon olive oil

Directions:

Combine the yogurt, lemon juice, chili powder, salt, black pepper and soy sauce.

Pour this mixture over chicken and rub gently on all sides of chicken, cover with plastic sheet.

Leave to rest for 60 minutes in the fridge.

In your instant pot add oil and place chicken, cover with the lid and leave to prepare for 20 minutes on manual mode, then flip the side and leave to cook again for another 20 minutes.

Transfer into serving the dish and serve with your desired sauce.

STUFFED BELL PEPPERS

Preparation Time: 10 minutes   Cooking time: 35 minutes   Servings: 4

Ingredients:

4 green bell peppers	2 tomatoes, chopped	3 tablespoon lemon juice
1 cup feta cheese	1 teaspoon black pepper	3-4 tablespoons olive oil
1 teaspoon salt	1 teaspoon garlic powder	

Directions:

Grease instant pot with olive oil.

Cut the peppers from the stem.

In a medium bowl add feta cheese, tomatoes, salt, black pepper, garlic powder, lemon juice and combine well.
Fill peppers with feta mixture and place into instant pot. Lock the lid.
Adjust your pot on slow cook mode. Cook for 35 minutes.
Serve and enjoy.

WHITE BEANS CURRY

Preparation Time: 5 minutes   Cooking Time: 50 minutes   Servings: 4

Ingredients:

1 cup white beans, soaked
1 cup broccoli, florets
2 lemons, thinly sliced
1 onion, chopped
1 teaspoon chili powder

½ teaspoon salt
4-5 garlic cloves, chopped
3 cup chicken broth
4 tablespoons cooking oil

Directions:

Adjust your instant pot on sauté mode.
Heat oil and add onion, sauté until it becomes glassy.
Now add garlic, chili powder, salt and fry for 1-2 minutes.
Stir in white beans, lemon, broccoli and chicken broth, cover and leave to prepare for 50 minutes on slow cook mode.
Transfer into serving the dish and serve.

CHICKEN, ORZO AND POTATOES

Preparation Time: 5 minutes   Cooking Time: 45 minutes   Servings: 4

Ingredients:

1 cup white orzo
1 carrot, sliced
1/2 cup parmesan cheese grated
3 medium potatoes, diced
1 onion, chopped
2 tomatoes, chopped

1 teaspoon chili powder
½ teaspoon salt
4-5 garlic cloves, chopped
3 cup chicken broth
4 tablespoons cooking oil

Directions:

Adjust instant pot on sauté mode.
In your instant pot heat oil and add onion, sauté until becomes tender.
Stir in potatoes, carrot, orzo, chicken broth, salt, chili powder, garlic, and tomatoes.
Cover and leave to prepare for 45 minutes on slow cook mode. Top with parmesan cheese.
Serve hot and enjoy.

LENTIL TACOS

Preparation Time: 15 minutes Cooking Time: 20 minutes Servings: 5-6

Ingredients:

2 cups black lentil
1 cup sour cream
1 large onion, sliced
2 tomatoes, chopped
½ teaspoon chili powder
½ teaspoon cumin powder
1 teaspoon garlic paste
1 teaspoon black pepper
½ teaspoon salt
2 cups water
1 cup chicken broth
4 tablespoons sunflower oil
1 bunch fresh cilantro, chopped
3 tablespoons lemon juice
10-12 corn tortillas

Directions:

Tune instant pot on manual mode.

Transfer lentil with garlic, cumin powder, chili powder, salt, black pepper, oil, vegetable broth and water in the instant pot.

Close and leave to cook for 20 minutes.

Now place tortilla and top with 3-4 tablespoons cooked lentil, onion, tomatoes, cilantro and sour cream.

Repeat with remaining tortillas. Serve with lemon slices and enjoy.

BUTTERNUT SQUASH RISOTTO

Preparation Time: 10 minutes Cooking Time: 20 minutes Servings: 4

Ingredients:

1 cup rice
1 cup butternut squash, chopped
½ cup baby spinach
1 red bell pepper, chopped
1 yellow bell pepper, chopped
1 large onion, sliced
1 teaspoon garlic paste
1 teaspoon black pepper
½ teaspoon salt
2 cups vegetable broth
4 tablespoons cooking oil

Directions:

Keep the instant pot on sauté mode.

Fry onion, till lightly tanned. Add in garlic paste, bell peppers, squash, salt, spinach and fry for 1-2 minutes.

Stir in vegetable broth and season with salt.

Adjust instant pot on manual mode and close the lid.

Leave to cook for 20 minutes.

Serve while still hot with some parmesan shavings.

BUFFALO CHICKEN WINGS

Preparation time: 5 minutes   Cooking time: 15 minutes   Servings: 4

Ingredients:

2 lbs. chicken wings
1 lb. trimmed celery
For the coating:
4 tablespoons honey
4 tablespoons hot sauce

4 tablespoons tomato puree
3 teaspoons salt
For the sauce:
1 tablespoon fresh chopped parsley
1 cup Greek yogurt

Directions:

Turn on the instant pot and place a cup of water inside as well as the steamer basket.
If the wings are still in whole pieces, separate out each and slice through the skin all the way to the joint. Place all of the wings into the steamer basket. Close and then lock the lid of your instant pot and turn the heat up so that it is on high. When the pressure is reached you can turn it down a little, but maintain the pressure. Cook for 10 minutes. While the wings are cooking, take out a bowl and combine the salt, tomato puree, honey, and hot sauce. Mix well so that everything is combined. After the 10 minutes, open the lid and coat the chicken with the prepared coating. Arrange the wings on baking sheet and broil for 5 minutes. In the meantime, prepare the sauce. Serve hot chicken wings with sauce.

PASTA FAGGIOLI

Preparation time: 5 minutes   Cooking time: 20 minutes   Servings: 4

Ingredients:

1 ½ cups white beans, dried, soaked overnight
2 tablespoons olive oil
2 cups chopped onions
1 tablespoon chopped garlic
2 chopped celery ribs
1 bay leaf
2 chopped carrots

1 ½ teaspoons basil, dried
5 cups water, boiling
1/4 teaspoons red pepper flakes
3 tablespoons tomato paste
1 cup shell pasta
1 teaspoon salt
1 tablespoon balsamic vinegar
¼ cup shredded cheese

Directions:

In the instant pot, heat up the oil before adding the onion and letting it soften for 2 minutes.
Add the garlic in next and cook for 30 seconds. Add in the boiling water, beans, spices, and the rest of the veggies. Lock the lid on the instant and then bring it to a high pressure.
Reduce the heat a bit and cook the meal for about 5 minutes.
When done you can allow the pressure to reduce a bit.
Use a quick pressure release method and open the lid.
Remove bay leaf before stirring in the pasta and tomato paste. Cook for another 7 minutes to finish off the pasta. Sprinkle with cheese. Serve after.

SUCCULENT LAMB SHANKS

Preparation time: 5 minutes   Cooking time: 35minutes   Servings: 4-6

Ingredients:

2lb. lamb shanks
10 peeled garlic cloves
1 tablespoon olive oil
½ cup port wine
½ cup chicken stock

1 tablespoon tomato paste
1 tablespoon butter
½ teaspoon rosemary, dried
1 teaspoon balsamic vinegar
Salt and pepper, to taste

Directions:

Take the extra fat from the lamb shanks and then season with pepper and salt.
Heat up the oil in the instant pot before adding the shanks. Brown them on all sides.
Once the shanks are almost done you can add the garlic and cook for 1 minute.
Add the rosemary, tomato paste, port, and stock. Close the instant pot and then bring it up to a high pressure.
Reduce the heat a bit to stabilize the pressure and then cook for about 30 minutes.
After this time, take the cooker from the heat and then allow the pressure to release. Take the shanks out before returning the pot to a high heat.
Boil the liquid for about 5 minutes to get it to thicken into a sauce.
Whisk in the butter before adding the vinegar. Serve this sauce on top of the lamb and enjoy.

JAMBALAYA

Preparation time: 5 minutes   Cooking time: 20 minutes   Servings: 4

Ingredients:

8 oz. sliced sausage
½ tablespoon oil
8 oz. chicken breast
8 oz. shrimp
½ teaspoon dried thyme
1 teaspoon creole seasoning
1 dash cayenne pepper
1 chopped onion
1 chopped green bell pepper

3 minced garlic cloves
1 chopped jalapeno pepper
3 sliced celery stalks
1 dash hot sauce
2 cups canned tomatoes
1 cup white rice
3 tablespoons fresh minced parsley
1 cup chicken broth

Directions:

Take out the instant pot and turn it to the Browning mode. Add in the shrimp, sausage, and chicken. Stir well. Sprinkle the meats with the half of cayenne, thyme, and seasoning. Cook it all together for 5 minutes, stirring often. Continue to cook until the meats are done. Use a slotted spoon and then set aside. Add in the celery, peppers, garlic, and onion along with the rest of the seasonings. Cook this for 5 minutes or until the vegetables are done. Add the broth, tomatoes, and rice. Place the cover on top and bring it to a high pressure. Cook it for 8 minutes. After this is done release the pressure and then add the parsley along with the cooked meat. Cover and allow to stand for 5 minutes. Serve warm.

Rich Minestrone soup

Preparation Time: 12 minutes   Cooking Time: 6 minutes   Servings: 6

Ingredients:

28 oz. fresh tomato, finely chopped
15 oz. cannellini beans, soaked and cooked
4 cups of vegetable broth
1 cup of pasta, gluten free
2 stalks of celery, finely chopped
1 large carrot, diced
1 large onion, diced

½ cup of fresh spinach
1/3 cup of parmesan cheese, grated
2 tablespoons of olive oil
1 bay leaf
1 teaspoon of dry basil
3 cloves of garlic, peeled and minced
Salt and black pepper, to taste

Directions:

Heat the olive oil in an instant pot and sauté in it the celery with onion, carrot, garlic and celery for 5 minutes.
Add in the basil with a pinch of salt and pepper then stir in the tomato with the rest of the ingredients except
for the cheese. Cover the pot and set it on high pressure then cook it for 6 minutes.
Once the time is up, allow the soup to sit for 2 min then release the pressure.
Stir the cheese into the soup then serve it warm and enjoy.

Bean chicken chili

Preparation Time: 10 minutes   Cooking Time: 30 minutes   Servings: 6

Ingredients:

1 lb .dry navy beans, soaked overnight
6 chicken thighs, boneless
14 oz. of tomato, diced
7 oz. of green chilies, seeded and chopped
4 cups of chicken broth, gluten free
2 cups of onion, finely chopped
3 tablespoons vegetable shortening

2 tablespoons cassava flour
2 teaspoons chili powder
1 teaspoon cumin
½ teaspoon dry oregano
4 cloves of garlic, peeled and minced
Salt and black pepper, to taste

Directions:

Drain the beans from the soaking liquid and stir it into an instant pot with the rest of the ingredients.
Cover pot and press the key
(Bean/chili) then let it cook for 30 minutes.
Once the time is up, allow the chili to sit for 15 min then release the pressure.
Transfer the chili to a large serving bowl and allow it to cool down and thicken for 30 then serve it warm
and enjoy.

REFRIED BEANS

Preparation Time: 10 min   Cooking Time: 45 min   Servings 6 to 8

Ingredients:

3 tablespoons vegetable shortening
1 lb. dry pinto beans, soaked overnight
1 ½ cup of onion, finely chopped
4 cups of water
4 cups of chicken broth, gluten free

1 ½ teaspoons of cumin
4 cloves of garlic, peeled and minced
1 jalapeno, seeded and finely chopped
Salt and pepper, to taste

Directions:

Stir all the ingredients in an instant pot and season it with a pinch of salt and pepper.
Cover the pot and press the button (Bean/chili) then cook it for 45 minutes on high pressure.
Once the time is up, release the pressure naturally and allow the bean cool down completely.
Serve after.

CUBAN PORK

Preparation Time: 10 min   Cooking Time: 2 h   Servings 12

Ingredients:

6 lb. pork roast, cut into 2-inch pieces
1 onion, thinly sliced
1 cup orange juice

2 tablespoons garlic, peeled and minced
2 tablespoons of olive oil
Salta and pepper, to taste

Directions:

Season the roast with some salt and pepper. Heat the olive oil in an instant pot and brown in it the roast from all sides. Whisk the orange juice with garlic in a bowl and pour it all over the roast with onion then cover the pot and cook for 2 h on high pressure. Once the time is up, release the pressure using the natural method and shred the roast. Stir the roast back into the pot with the rest of the juices then serve it warm and enjoy.

CHICKEN SALSA

Preparation Time: 15 min   Cooking Time: 15 min   Servings: 4

Ingredients:

1 lb. of chicken breasts, skinless and boneless
1 ½ cup of salsa

½ teaspoon of onion powder
½ teaspoon of garlic powder

Directions:

Stir all the ingredients in the pot and cover it. Press the Poultry button and cook it for 15 minutes on high pressure. Once the time is up, use the quick method to release the pressure then shred the chicken.
Serve your chicken salsa with tortillas and enjoy.

Coconut Chicken

Preparation Time: 15 minutes   Cooking Time: 15   Servings: 6

Ingredients:

4 lb. chicken breasts
8 oz. of coconut milk
¼ cup of fresh lemon juice

1 tablespoon of curry powder
1 teaspoon of turmeric
Salta and pepper to taste

Directions:

Combine the coconut milk with turmeric, curry and lemon juice in a small bowl.
Pour some of the mix in the instant pot and lower in it the chicken breast then pour on it the rest of the mix.
Cover the pot, and press the Poultry option and cook it for 15 minutes on high pressure.
Once the time is up, drain the chicken and shred it then stir it back into the pot with the rest of the juices.
Serve your shredded chicken with desired steamed veggies and enjoy.

Asian Beef

Preparation Time: 10 minutes   Cooking Time: 35 minutes   Servings: 6

Ingredients:

5 lb. beef pot roast
½ cup of water
¼ cup fish sauce
2 tablespoons of fresh ginger, peeled and

1 tablespoon of granulated sugar
3 cloves of garlic, crushed
1 teaspoon of red wine vinegar
Salt and pepper, to taste

Directions:

Season the chuck roast with some salt and pepper and stir it into an instant pot with the rest of the ingredients.
Cover the pot and cook the roast for 35 minutes on high pressure.
Once the time is up, drain the roast and shred it then stir it back into the pot with the rest of the juices.
Serve your shredded roast warm and enjoy.

Cabbage Congee

Preparation Time: 10 minutes   Cooking Time: 20 minutes   Servings: 6

Ingredients:

1 lb. chicken, minced
10 cups of homemade bone broth
4 cups Savoy cabbage, shredded
1 ½ cups short grain rice
3 ribs of celery, thinly sliced
2 radishes, diced
1 large shallot, peeled and finely chopped

1 small turnip, peeled and diced
1 tablespoon of vegetable shortening
2 tablespoons of fresh ginger, peeled and grated
Salt and black pepper, to taste

Directions:

Melt the shortening in an instant pot and sauté in it the celery with radish, turnip, and shallot for 3 minutes.

Stir in the broth with chicken, rice, and ginger with a pinch of salt.

Cover the pot and set to Porridge option. Cook for 20 minutes and then release the pressure naturally.

Once the time is up, drain the chicken and shred it then stir back into the soup.

Stir the cabbage into the pot and cook until wilted and then adjust its seasoning.

Serve while still hot and enjoy.

CHILI BEEF STEW

Preparation Time: 10 minutes   Cooking Time: 45 minutes   Servings: 4

Ingredients:

1 lb. lean beef, minced
29 oz. of fresh tomato, diced
5 carrots, sliced
3 stalks celery, finely chopped
1 green bell pepper, seeded and diced
1 onion, finely chopped
1 habanero pepper, seeded and finely chopped

1 tablespoon chili powder
1 tablespoon avocado oil
4 cloves garlic, peeled and minced
1 ½ teaspoons cumin
1 teaspoon paprika
Salt and pepper, to taste

Directions:

Heat the oil in an instant pot and sauté in it the garlic with onion for 2 minutes.

Add in the beef and cook it for 5 minutes then stir in the rest of the ingredients and cover the pot.

Press the Meat/Stew button and cook the stew for 35 minutes on high pressure.

Once the time is up, release the pressure naturally then serve your stew warm and enjoy.

CHICKEN TIGHT STEW

Preparation Time: 10 minutes   Cooking Time: 30 minutes   Servings: 6

Ingredients:

1 ½ lb. chicken thighs, cut into bite pieces
15 oz. tomato sauce
1 cup coconut cream
1 onion, peeled and diced
2 tablespoon butter
5 cloves garlic, peeled and minced
1 teaspoon turmeric

1 teaspoon garam masala
1 teaspoon coriander powder
1 teaspoon paprika
¼ teaspoon cayenne pepper
¼ teaspoon cumin
Salt and pepper, to taste

Directions:

Melt the butter in an instant pot and sauté onion in butter for 8 minutes.

Add in the ginger with garlic and cook them for 30 seconds.

Add the chicken with spices and brown them.

Stir in the rest of the ingredients except for the coconut cream and cover the pot.

Press the Poultry button and cook it for 15 minutes on high pressure.

Once the time is up, stir in the coconut cream then serve your stew warm and enjoy.

LENTILS CHILI

Preparation Time: 15 minutes   Cooking Time: 10 minutes   Servings: 8 to 10

Ingredients:

1 lb. red lentils
1 lb. red bell pepper, seeded and chopped
29 oz. fresh tomato, peeled diced
10 oz. onion, finely chopped
7 cups water
3 oz. dates, pitted
4 tablespoons apple cider vinegar

1 ½ tablespoons chili powder
1 ½ tablespoons fresh parsley, finely chopped
1 ½ tablespoons fresh oregano, finely chopped
8 cloves garlic, minced
Salt and pepper, to taste

Directions:

Combine the garlic with bell pepper, dates, 1 cup of water and tomato in a food processor and process until smooth.

Transfer the mix to an instant pot and stir in the rest of the ingredients.

Cover the pot and cook it for 10 minutes on high pressure.

Once the time is up, release the pressure naturally.

Serve the stew and enjoy.

FALL OFF PORK RIBS

Preparation Time: 15 minutes   Cooking Time: 35 minutes   Servings: 10

Ingredients:

For Ribs:
5 lb. pork ribs, trimmed and cut into sections
For the dry rub:
1 ½ tablespoons Himalayan salt
1 tablespoon honey
1 teaspoon paprika
1 teaspoon baking powder
1 teaspoon onion powder
½ teaspoon ground coriander
½ teaspoon allspice

For sauce:
½ cup of water
½ cup of ketchup
2 tablespoons red wine vinegar
2 tablespoons any sweetener
½ tablespoon ground allspice
½ tablespoon ground mustard
½ teaspoon onion powder
2 tablespoons cornstarch (dissolved in water)

Method:

Combine all the dry rub ingredients in a small bowl. Rub the ribs with them.

Place the ribs in an instant pot and set it aside.

Combine all of the sauce ingredients, except the starch, in a small bowl and pour over the ribs.

Cover the pot and cook the ribs for 35 minutes on high pressure.

Once the time is up, drain the ribs and set them aside. Whisk the starch into the sauce and sauté it until it thickens.

Pour the sauce all over the ribs and serve.

MEXICAN MEATLOAF

Preparation Time: 20 minutes　　　Cooking Time: 35 minutes　　　Servings: 6

Ingredients:

2 lb. lean beef, minced
1 cup tomato, finely chopped
1 large yellow onion, finely chopped
¼ cup tapioca starch
1 egg

1 teaspoon onion powder
1 teaspoon cumin
1 teaspoon garlic powder
1 teaspoon chili powder
Salt and pepper, to taste

Directions:

Mix all the ingredients in a large bowl and stir until combined.

Pour 1 cup of water in the bottom of an instant pot then place in it a steamer basket on the trivet.

Cover the meatloaf tightly and wrap it with a piece of foil then place it in the steaming basket. Cover the pot and cook the meatloaf for 35 minutes on high pressure.

Once the time is up, release the pressure naturally.

Serve the meatloaf with some sauce and enjoy.

ASIAN RIBS STEW

Preparation Time: 10 minutes　　　Cooking Time: 30 minutes　　　Servings: 4

Ingredients:

1 ¾ lb. short ribs, boneless
1 large onion, finely chopped
1 carrot, sliced
4 tablespoons soy sauce
4 tablespoons mirin

2 tablespoons brown sugar
1 tablespoon sesame oil
2 cloves garlic, minced
Salt and pepper, to taste

Directions:

Season the ribs with some salt and pepper. Heat the oil in an instant pot and sauté in it the carrots with onion for 5 minutes. Stir in the rest of the ingredients and cover the pot. Bring it to a high pressure.

Cook the stew for 30 minutes on high pressure. Use a quick pressure release method to let the steam out.

Serve while still hot.

PULLED PORK ROAST

Preparation Time: 10 minutes   Cooking Time: 1 h   Servings: 6

Ingredients:

4 lb. pork shoulder
1 cup beef broth, gluten free
1 large onion, thinly sliced

4 cloves garlic, peeled and sliced
Salt and pepper, to taste

Directions:

Combine the onion with garlic and broth in an instant pot.
Season the pork shoulder with some salt and pepper then place it in the pot
Lock the lid and cook the pork on high pressure for 1 hour.
Once the time is up, release the pressure naturally and drain the pork shoulder.
Shred the pork and serve it your favorite BBQ sauce.

CHICKEN BBQ POT

Preparation Time: 10 minutes   Cooking Time: 15 minutes   Servings: 6

Ingredients:

3 lb. chicken wings
1 cup preferred BBQ sauce
4 lemon slices

1 ½ tablespoons tapioca starch
1 clove of garlic, finely chopped

Directions:

Season the chicken wings with some salt and pepper. Arrange the chicken on a baking sheet and broil for 5 minutes.
Stir the rest of the ingredients into an instant pot. Add the chicken wings and cover. Cook on high for 10 minutes.
Once the time is up, adjust the seasoning and serve while still hot.

BRAISED BEEF AND CARROTS

Preparation Time: 10 minutes   Cooking Time: 1 h 10 minutes   Servings: 6

Ingredients:

4 lb. beef chuck roast
2 cups of bone broth, gluten free
6 small carrots, peeled
1 onion, peeled

2 tablespoons coconut oil
1 tablespoon Italian seasoning
1 teaspoon garlic powder
Salt and pepper, to taste

Method:

Season the roast with some salt and pepper and place aside.
Melt the coconut oil in an instant pot and sauté in it the onion for 5 minutes.

Add the broth and seasoned roast.

Cover the pot and cook the roast for 1 hour on high pressure.

Once the time is up, release the pressure naturally and stir in the rest of the ingredients. Sauté them for 10 minutes.

Serve while still hot.

RICE PILAF

Preparation Time: 5 minutes   Cooking Time: 8 minutes   Servings: 4

Ingredients:

1 lb. white mushroom, sliced
1 lb. green beans, finely chopped
2 ½ cups chicken stock, gluten free
2 cups kale, finely chopped
2 cups short grain rice
1 cup leftover meat, any kind, roughly chopped

2 potatoes, peeled and diced
2 carrots, finely chopped
2 tablespoons soy sauce
1 tablespoon rice wine
1 tablespoon vegetable oil
1 tablespoon oyster sauce
Salt and pepper, to taste

Directions:

Combine all the ingredients in an instant pot and season them with some salt and pepper.

Cover the pot and press on the "Bean/Chili" button and cook for 8 minutes on high pressure.

Once the time is up, release the pressure naturally and open the lid.

Serve your pilaf rice warm with some fresh salad.

MUSHROOM RISOTTO

Preparation Time: 10 minutes   Cooking Time: 8 minutes   Servings: 6

Ingredients:

3 cups vegetable broth
1 cup Arborio rice
4 oz. mushroom, finely chopped
½ cup yellow onion, minced
4 tablespoons grated parmesan

1 tablespoon butter
1 tablespoon olive oil
3 cloves of garlic, minced
Salt and white pepper, to taste

Directions:

Heat the oil in an instant pot and sauté in it the garlic with onion for 3 minutes.

Stir in the rest of the ingredients except for the lemon juice.

Lock the lid and cook the risotto for 5 minutes on high pressure.

Once the time is up, release the pressure naturally.

Stir the lemon juice into the rice and adjust its seasoning.

Serve while still hot.

*I*NSTANT JAMBALAYA

Preparation Time: 10 minutes   Cooking Time: 4 minutes   Servings: 6

Ingredients:

12 oz. sausages, sliced
4 cups chicken broth
2 cups long grain rice
2 green bell peppers, finely chopped
2 red bell peppers, finely chopped
2 small onions, finely chopped

2 tablespoons tomato paste
2 tablespoons olive oil
1 tablespoons Cajun seasoning
4 cloves garlic, minced
Salt and pepper, to taste

Directions:

Heat the oil in an instant pot. Cook the onion and peppers for 5 minutes.
Stir in the rest of the ingredients and season them with salt and pepper.
Cover the pot and cook the jambalaya for 4 minutes on high pressure.
Once the time is up, adjust the seasoning jambalaya.
Serve while still hot.

*R*OASTED CHICKEN POT

Preparation Time: 10 minutes   Cooking Time: 25 minutes   Servings: 10

Ingredients:

4 lb. whole chicken
1 ½ cups beef broth
2 tablespoons lemon juice
6 cloves garlic, peeled

1 tablespoon coconut oil
1 teaspoon smoked paprika
Salt and pepper, to taste

Directions:

Mix the garlic with paprika and coconut oil in a small bowl. Rub the chicken with it.
Place the chicken in an instant pot and stir in the rest of the ingredients.
Lock the lid and select Poultry option.Cook for 25 minutes and use a natural pressure release method.
Serve while still hot.

*S*AUSAGE STEW

Preparation Time: 10 minutes   Cooking Time: 10 minutes   Servings: 6

Ingredients:

20 oz. sausages, cooked and thickly sliced
5 cups vegetable broth
2 cups red beans, soaked overnight

¾ cup of red bell peppers, seeded and finely chopped
1 cup onions, finely chopped
1 tablespoon tomato paste

1 tablespoon olive oil
3 cloves garlic, minced

1 teaspoon dry parsley
Salt and pepper, to taste

Directions:

Hcat the oil in an instant pot and sauté in it the red bell pepper with onion for 5 minutes.
Stir in the rest of the ingredients and cover the pot.
Cook on high pressure for 5 minutes. Use a quick pressure release and open the lid.
Adjust the seasonings and serve while still hot with toasted bread slices.

CARROT RISOTTO

Preparation Time: 10 minutes
Cooking Time: 12 minutes

Servings: 4

Ingredients:

3 ¾ cups vegetable broth
5 carrots, diced
1 ½ cups Arborio rice
1 ½ cups butternut squash, diced
1 white onion, finely chopped

¼ cup parmesan cheese, grated
1 tablespoon olive oil
3 cloves garlic, finely chopped
Salt and pepper, to taste

Directions:

Heat the olive oil in an instant pot and sauté in it the carrot with butternut squash and onion for 5 minutes.
Add in the rice with garlic and cook for 1 minute.
Stir in the rest of the ingredients except for the cheese and season with salt and pepper, to taste.
Lock the lid and cook on high pressure for 7 minutes. Use a quick pressure release method.
Stir in the cheese and serve while still hot.

CHICKEN TIKKA MASALA

Preparation Time: 10 minutes   Cooking Time: 40 minutes   Servings: 6

Ingredients:

6 chicken thighs
28 oz. fresh tomato, diced
15 oz. coconut milk
1 yellow onion, peeled and diced
3 tablespoons tomato paste

2 tablespoons olive oil
2 teaspoons garlic, minced
1 ½ teaspoons Garam Masala
Salt and pepper, to taste

Directions:

Heat the olive oil in an instant pot and brown in it the chicken for 2 minutes on each side. Place the chicken aside. Stir the onion in the same pot and cook it for 3 minutes. Add the garlic and cook it for another minute. Stir in the rest of the ingredients and
cover the pot. Cook for 30 minutes on high pressure. Once the time is up, release the pressure naturally. Serve while still hot.

ASIAN BEEF WITH NOODLES

Preparation Time: 20 minutes   Cooking Time: 18 minutes   Servings: 4

Ingredients:

½ lb. beef, sliced
7 oz. noodles
2 potatoes, cut into chunks
1 large carrot, sliced
1 cup green beans, trimmed and cut into
2-inch pieces
1 cup beef broth

3 tablespoons soy sauce
3 tablespoons mirin
2 tablespoons sake
1 tablespoon vegetable oil
1 tablespoon brown sugar
Salt and pepper, to taste

Directions:

Blanche the beans in a pot of salted boiling water for 3 minutes. Drain the green beans and set them aside.
Heat the oil in an instant pot and stir into it the rest of the ingredients.
Press the Meat/Stew button and cook the stew for 15 minutes on high pressure.
Once the time is up, release the pressure naturally.
Stir the beans into the stew and adjust its seasoning.
Serve your stew warm and enjoy.

LAMB STEW

Preparation Time: 15 minutes   Cooking Time: 20 minutes   Servings: 4

Ingredients:

2 lb. lamb shoulder, trimmed and cut into
chunks
2 cups fresh tomato, diced
1 cup water
½ cup plain yogurt
1 large white onion, finely chopped
3 tablespoons vegetable oil

2 teaspoons Garam masala
2 teaspoons paprika
1 teaspoon cumin
1 teaspoon turmeric
2 cloves garlic, peeled
Salt and pepper, to taste

Directions:

Combine the yogurt with garam masala, turmeric, paprika, cumin and cayenne pepper in a food processor.
Process until smooth. Transfer the mix into a zip lock bag and place aside.
Season the lamb with some salt and
pepper then place it in the ziplock bag. Let it sit in the marinade for few hours.
Combine the onion with tomato and garlic in a food processor, and process until smooth.
Pour the tomato mix with water in an instant pot with the lamb chunks and the rest of the marinade.
Cover the pot and cook the stew for 20 minutes on high pressure.
Release the pressure naturally to let the steam escape,
Adjust the seasonings and serve while still hot with some rice.

CHICKEN WITH LEMON SAUCE

Preparation Time: 10 minutes   Cooking Time 15 minutes   Servings: 6

Ingredients:

2 ½ lb. chicken breasts halves
2/3 cup of chicken broth
2 eggs
2 ½ tablespoon tapioca starch
2 tablespoons fresh lemon juice

1 tablespoon butter
1 tablespoon olive oil
4 slices lemon
Salt and pepper, to taste

Directions:

Season the chicken with some salt and pepper.

Whisk the eggs with starch in a small bowl and set aside.

Heat the olive oil in a skillet.

Dip the chicken breasts halves in the egg mix and fry them in the skillet for 2 minutes on each side.

Once the time is up, transfer the chicken into an instant pot with the rest of the ingredients and lock the lid.

Cook the chicken for 15 minutes on high pressure. Use a quick pressure release.

Serve your chicken warm and enjoy.

CHICKEN BIRYANI

Preparation Time: 10 minutes   Cooking Time: 20 minutes   Servings: 4

Ingredients:

10.5 oz. basmati rice
4 cups white onion, sliced
1 cup thick coconut milk
¼ cup cashews
4 tablespoons vegetable shortening
3 tablespoons plain curd

1 ½ tablespoons Biryani masala
5 green chilies, seeded and finely chopped
2 inches ginger, peeled and grated
½ teaspoon turmeric powder
Salt and pepper, to taste

Directions:

Mix the garlic with ginger and chilies in a food blender and blend them smoothly.

Place the rice in a bowl and cover it with water. Let it soak for 30 minutes.

Heat the shortening in an instant pot and sauté in it the ginger mix with chicken, turmeric and Biryani masala for 3 minutes.

Mix the water with coconut milk then pour it into the instant pot and bring them to a boil.

Cover the pot then cook it for 15 minutes on high pressure.

Once the time is up, release the pressure naturally then stir in the curd with cashews.

Use a quick pressure release method.

Adjust the seasoning of your Biryani. Serve while still hot.

PLAIN PORK CHOPS

Preparation Time: 15 minutes   Cooking Time: 14 minutes   Servings: 4

Ingredients:

4 thick pork chops
1 head cabbage, sliced
¾ cup beef stock
2 teaspoons arrowroot powder

1 tablespoon vegetable oil
1 teaspoon fennel seeds
Salt and pepper, to taste

Directions:

Season the pork chops with some salt, pepper, and fennel seeds. Heat the oil in an instant pot and brown in it the pork chops for 3 minutes on each side. Drain the chops and set them aside.

Arrange the sliced cabbage in the instant pot and place the pork chops on it. Pour over the stock.

Cook the pork chops for 8 min on high pressure. Use a natural pressure release.

Drain the pork chops and cabbage and set them aside.

Whisk the arrowroot powder into the rest of the juices and simmer it until it thickens slightly.

Serve with pork chops and cabbage while still hot.

SPANISH PAELLA

Preparation time: 5 minutes   Cooking Time: 10 minutes   Servings: 4

Ingredients:

6 cups fish stock
2 cups short grain rice
2 cups mixed shellfish (shrimp, mussels and clams)
1 ¾ cups vegetable stock
1 cup of mixed seafood (white fish, squid, scallops)

1 yellow onion, finely chopped
1 green bell pepper, diced
1 red bell pepper, diced
2 tablespoons olive oil
1 pinch of saffron threads
Salt and pepper, to taste

Directions:

Heat the oil in an instant pot. Select Saute option and cook the peppers with onion for 4 minutes.

Stir in the rest of the ingredients and cover the pot. Cook for 6 minutes on high pressure.

Once the time is up, release the pressure naturally. Serve while still hot with toasted bread slices.

RICE, PORK, AND VEGETABLES

Preparation Time: 10 minutes   Cooking Time: 14 minutes   Servings: 8

Ingredients:

8 pork chops
4 cups tomato, diced
2 cups water

2 cups rice
6 tablespoons green bell pepper, seeded and diced

4 tablespoons onion, finely chopped

2 tablespoons olive oil

Salt and pepper, to taste

Directions:

Heat the oil in an instant pot. Select Saute brown the pork chops for 3 minutes per side.

Stir in the tomato with rice and cook them for 3 minutes.

Add the remaining ingredients and season to taste.

Cover the pot and cook them for 9 minutes on high pressure.

Use a quick pressure release and serve while still hot.

PULLED TOMATO CHICKEN

Preparation Time: 10 minutes   Cooking Time: 30 minutes   Servings: 4

Ingredients:

1 ½ lb. chicken breasts

14 oz. fresh tomato, crushed

¼ cup chicken broth

4 chilies, seeded

2 teaspoons sugar

2 cloves garlic, crushed

1 teaspoon onion powder

1 teaspoon cumin

Salt and pepper, to taste

Directions:

Combine the broth with chilies in a food processor and blend them smoothly.

Transfer the chilies mix with the rest of the ingredients into an instant pot.

Lock the lid, select Manual, and cook on high pressure for 30 minutes.

Once the time is up, release the pressure naturally and drain the chicken. Shred it up and place back in the pot.

Adjust seasonings and serve while still hot.

IRRESISTIBLE GOAT CURRY

Preparation Time: 10 minutes   Cooking Time: 1 h   Servings: 6

Ingredients:

2 lb. goat meat

½ lb. potatoes, halved

28 oz. fresh tomato, diced

2 onions, diced

½ cup water

2 tablespoons avocado oil

1 ½-inch fresh ginger, peeled, minced

1 tablespoon coriander powder

3 cloves garlic, minced

1 teaspoon chili powder

1 teaspoon garam masala

1 teaspoon turmeric

1 teaspoon cumin

4 whole cloves

Salta and pepper, to taste

Directions:

Heat the oil in an instant pot. Select Saute and brown the goat meat for 3 minutes.

Add in the garlic with onion with cloves and the rest of the spices.

Sauté for another 3 minutes. Stir in the rest of the ingredients.

Cover the pot and cook the curry for 45 minutes on high pressure.

Once the time is up, release the pressure naturally then adjust the seasoning of the stew.

Serve your goat curry warm.

VEGETABLE CURRY

Preparation time: 10 minutes   Cooking time: 35 minutes   Servings: 6

Ingredients:

1 teaspoon ground cinnamon
2 carrots, chopped
1 cup orange juice
1 14oz. can drained chickpeas
1 zucchini, sliced
1 red bell pepper, chopped
4 minced garlic cloves
1 tablespoon curry powder
1 onion, chopped
½ tablespoon sea salt

1 green bell pepper, chopped
¾ teaspoon cayenne pepper
1 medium cubed eggplant
1 teaspoon grated ginger
2 tablespoons raisins
¼ cup blanched almond
2 teaspoons ground turmeric
1 sweet potato, peeled and cubed
10 oz. spinach
6 tablespoons olive oil

Directions:

In the instant pot, combine sweet potatoes and carrots. Lock the lid and cook for 5 minutes at high pressure.

Use a quick pressure release method to open the lid.

Add raisins, orange juice and chickpeas. Lock the lid and cook for 12 minutes on high pressure.

Use a quick pressure release and open the lid. Add the remaining ingredients and high pressure for 6 minutes.

Use a quick pressure release for the last time and open the lid.

Serve vegetable curry with some steamed Jasmine rice.

Enjoy.

RICE STUFFED PEPPERS

Preparation time: 10 minutes   Cooking time 50 minutes   Servings: 6

Ingredients:

1 can fire roasted diced tomatoes
2 tablespoons ketchup
1 teaspoon ground black pepper
1/3 cup water

1 cup cooked rice
1 teaspoon Worcestershire sauce
6 green bell peppers (seeds and tops removed and place aside)

Directions:

Heat the oil in an instant pot at Sate option. Make a mixture of tomatoes, ketchup, black pepper, Worcestershire sauce, and rice. Stuff the peppers with prepared mixture. Arrange the peppers in the pot and close with reserved tops. Pour over water or vegetable broth, just 2-uinches of liquid.

Cook for 45 minutes on low pressure. Use a quick pressure release and serve while still hot.

SOUTHERN STYLE CABBAGE

Preparation time: 20 minutes   Cooking time: 10 minutes   Servings: 4

Ingredients:

8 slices bacon
2 cups chicken broth
¼ cup butter

1 head cabbage, cored
Salt and pepper, to taste

Directions:

Chop the cabbage.
Cook the bacon in instant pot at Saute function.
Add butter and let it melt completely.
Add chopped cabbage to the pot and add chicken broth.
Season with salt and pepper.
Adjust the pot to high pressure then lower the heat to ensure the rocking motion is gentle.
Cook for 3 minutes.
Use a quick pressure release method.
Serve while still hot.

GOLDEN CHICKEN

Preparation time: 10 minutes   Cooking time: 20 minutes   Servings: 4

Ingredients:

12 skinless chicken wings
¼ teaspoon turmeric
½ teaspoon dry mustar
1 teaspoon smoked paprika
2 teaspoons ground pepper

½ teaspoon salt
½ cup ketchup
½ cup BBQ sauce
2 tablespoons melted butter
2 tablespoons vegetable oil

Directions:

Take out the Instant pot and turn on the "Sauté" setting. Once it has been heated for 5 minutes, you
Add the chicken wings. Do around 4-5 at a time.
Add in the vegetable oil and let it heat for 5 minutes.
Once the wings are golden, you can now put on the lid and turn on the Poultry' setting.
In the meantime, prepare the sauce; mix ketchup, butter, and BBQ sauce in a bowl.
Once the cooking cycle is done, use a natural pressure release.
Serve chicken with prepared sauce.

*I*TALIAN STYLE CHICKEN

Preparation time: 10 minutes   Cooking time: 10 minutes   Servings: 6

Ingredients:

4 Italian sausage links
1 tablespoon olive oil
1 chicken with skin off and cut up
1 onion, chopped
2 garlic cloves
2 green bell peppers

¾ teaspoon dried basil
1 14oz. can tomatoes, diced
Red pepper flakes, to taste
¼ teaspoon fennel seeds
Salt and pepper, to taste

Directions:

Heat the oil up in the instant pot.

While that is heating up, prick the sausages in a few places using a fork.

Add the chicken and the sausage into the instant pot and then cook them until they are browned on all sides.

Meanwhile, dice the onion, cut the peppers into strips, and mince the garlic.

Once the meats are browned, take them out of the cooker and set them to the side.

Add the garlic, green peppers, and onion to the cooker and let them cook for around 4 minutes. Add the vinegar and then stir around the browned bits in the cooker.

After this time, add in the red pepper, fennel, basil, tomatoes, sausages, and chicken.

Close the lid of the instant pot and bring it up to a full pressure.

Reduce the heat and cook for about 10 minutes.

Once done, release the pressure naturally and open the lid.

Adjust seasonings and serve warm.

*D*UCK STEW

Preparation time: 5 minutes   Cooking time: 10 minutes   Servings: 4

Ingredients:

1 cup green beans
1 tablespoon black pepper
½ cup carrots, shredded
2 tablespoons cornstarch
2 tablespoons chili powder

1 tablespoon honey
1 tablespoons orange juice
2 tablespoons lemon juice
2 cups chicken broth
1 cup duck breast, sliced

Directions:

Take all of the ingredients and add them into the prepared instant pot.

Place the lid on the instant pot and turn to a high setting.

Cook all the ingredients for 25 minutes.

Use a natural pressure release.

Serve while still hot.

FRIED CHICKEN LEGS

Preparation time: 10 minutes   Cooking time: 15 minutes   Servings: 4

Ingredients:

1 cup all-purpose flour
½ teaspoon flavored pepper
½ teaspoon poultry seasoning
¼ teaspoon garlic powder
½ teaspoon onion powder

½ cup milk
3 eggs
1 tablespoon honey
1lb. chicken legs

Directions:

Bring out a bowl and mix together all of the dry ingredients.

Coat the chicken with the prepared mix.

In a separate bowl, whisk the honey, milk, and eggs until they are well mixed. Dip the chicken into the eggs, and dip again into the flour mix.

Bring out the instant pot. Place some hot oil inside before adding the chicken and letting it brown.

Place the lid on top and let the chicken cook inside the cooker for about 15 minutes.

Serve the fried chicken with your favorite vegetables or fries.

Serve and enjoy.

SIMPLE JUICY STEAK

Preparation time: 5 minutes   Cooking time: 35 minutes   Servings: 4

Ingredients:

2 lb. flank steak
¼ cup apple cider vinegar
1 tablespoon Worcestershire sauce

½ cup olive oil
2 tablespoons onion soup mix

Directions:

Set Instant Pot to saute.

Add flank steak and brown on each side.

Add vinegar, Worcestershire, olive oil and onion soup mix.

Lock the lid.

Set on Meat/Stew setting or set manually for 35 minutes.

Use a quick pressure release method.

Serve steak with steamed veggies or oven baked potatoes.

Leftover Chicken rice casserole

Preparation time: 5 minutes   Cooking time: 7 minutes   Servings: 4

Ingredients:

1 ½ cups water
1 cup Italian dressing
9 oz. cooked shredded chicken (use leftovers)

4oz. shredded Cheddar cheese
Salt and pepper, to taste

Directions:

Coat Instant Pot with nonstick cooking spray.
Rinse the rice and place into the Instant Pot.
Pour water and Italian dressing into the Instant Pot.
Set to manual and cook for 7 minutes.
Cut the chicken into chunks. Once the rice has cooked do a quick release and open the Instant Pot.
Add the shredded cheese and the chicken in and stir well.
Adjust seasonings and serve while still hot.

Turkey, sauerkraut, and cranberries

Preparation time: 10 minutes   Cooking time: 40 minutes   Servings: 8

Ingredients:

2 cups sauerkraut, drained
¼ cup raisins
3 cloves garlic, chopped
4 lb. turkey wings or thighs
1 ½ cups fresh or frozen cranberries, divided
1 small preserved lemon, chopped and seeds removed

1 teaspoon ground cinnamon
½ tablespoon dried parsley
1 teaspoon dried thyme
1 teaspoon sea salt
1 cup apple cider
1 teaspoon arrowroot flour
2 teaspoons water

Directions:

Place the sauerkraut at the bottom of the pot. Scatter the raisins and garlic over evenly.
Place the turkey parts in the pot. Sprinkle 1 cup cranberries and preserved lemon over the turkey.
In a bowl, combine the ground cinnamon, parsley flakes, thyme, sea salt and apple cider and pour into the pot. Seal the lid of the instant pot and select Poultry setting for 25- 30 minutes.
Once the cooking time is over, release pressure naturally. Preheat the oven broiler in the meantime
Remove the turkey pieces from the pot and place them in an oven-proof casserole, then broil for around 5 minutes. Set the Instant Pot to Saute setting, then add in remaining ½ cup of cranberries
Prepare the arrowroot flour by combining the arrowroot flour with water.
Once the sauce begins to simmer, stir in the arrowroot flour mix and simmer until sauce is thickened.
Turn off the Instant Pot and serve the cranberry and sauerkraut sauce with the browned turkey parts.

ROASTED GARLIC CHICKEN

Preparation time: 5 minutes   Cooking time: 30 minutes   Servings: 4-6

Ingredients:

1-2 lb. chicken breasts or thighs
1 teaspoon sea salt
1 onion, diced
1 tablespoon avocado oil
5 garlic cloves, minced
½ cup organic chicken broth or homemade

1 teaspoon dried parsley
¼ teaspoon paprika
¼ cup white cooking wine
1 large lemon, juiced
3-4 teaspoons arrowroot flour

Directions:

Turn your Instant Pot onto the Saute feature and place in the diced onion and avocado oil.
Cook the onions for 5-10 minutes or until softened.
Add in the remaining ingredients except for the arrowroot flour and secure the lid on your Instant Pot.
Select the Poultry setting and lock the lid.
Allow cook time to complete, release steam valve to vent and then carefully remove the lid.
Mix ¼ cup cooking sauce with arrowroot flour and stir in the instant pot.
Simmer until thickened.
Serve while still hot.

VEGETABLE RISOTTO

Preparation time: 5 minutes   Cooking time: 10 minutes   Servings: 4

Ingredients:

2 tablespoons vegetable broth
½ cup finely chopped onion
3 cloves garlic, minced
1 cup diced acorn squash
1 cup diced eggplant
1 ½ cups Arborio rice
3 ½ cups chicken broth
½ white wine

1 teaspoon salt
½ teaspoon black pepper
1 teaspoon oregano
½ fresh chopped parsley
2 tablespoons grated parmesan
1 tablespoon butter
1 medium sized tomato, diced

Directions:

Heat the vegetable broth in instant pot on Saute option. Add the onion, garlic and cook for 3 minutes.
Add the squash and eggplant and stir well. Cook until soften.
Add the rice, and stir well. Add the chicken broth, wine, pepper, and oregano and stir well.
Close the lid and select Manual. Cook for 5 minutes.
Once Instant Pot finishes, carefully release the pressure.
Stir in parsley, parmesan, and butter. Cover and let is stand for 5 minutes.
Serve after.

Shepard's Pie

Preparation Time: 15 minutes   Cooking Time: 45 minutes   Servings: 6-8

Ingredients:

1 tablespoon olive oil
½ cup carrots, chopped
½ cup celery, chopped
½ red onion, chopped
3 garlic cloves, minced
1 red bell pepper, chopped
½ cup kale stemmed and chopped
2 cups mushrooms, sliced
½ teaspoon fresh thyme
2 tablespoons all-purpose flour

1 ½ - 2 cups vegetable broth
½ cup corn
½ cup peas
¾ cup dry green lentils
2 tablespoons grated Parmesan
1 ½ lb. potatoes washed thoroughly
1/3 cup almond milk
1 tablespoon butter
Salt and pepper, to taste

Directions:

Preheat oven to 3750F

Prick each potato with a fork or knife. Place the potatoes in instant pot with the larger potatoes on the bottom. Add enough water to cover half of the potatoes, but do not fill the instant cooker more than halfway up. Sprinkle with salt, cover, and seal, and bring to pressure. Cook at high pressure for 15-18 minutes. Turn off the cooker and allow the instant pot to release naturally. Drain.

While potatoes are cooking, in a large skillet over medium-high heat, add onions, celery, carrots, garlic, bell pepper, and kale. Cook for 3 minutes, and add mushrooms and thyme.

Continue cooking until vegetables are tender, about 10 minutes.

Sprinkle flour over vegetables and stir. Add vegetable broth in small amounts, until it becomes thin gravy. Add corn, peas, lentils, and parmesan. Simmer 5 minutes, adding more vegetable broth if needed. Mash the potatoes, adding in milk, earth balance, salt, and pepper to taste.

Pour lentil and veggie mixture into large casserole dish. Spoon potatoes on top and bake for 20 to 25 minutes. Serve after.

Stir Fried Shrimps

Preparation time: 5 minutes   Cooking time: 5 minutes   Servings: 4

Ingredients:

1 ½ cups shrimps
4-5 garlic cloves, chopped
1/2 teaspoon salt

1 teaspoon black pepper
3 tablespoons olive oil

Directions:

Heat oil in instant pot and add garlic cloves, sauté for 1 minute on sauté mode. Now add shrimps and fry until golden brown. Sprinkle salt and black pepper, mix thoroughly. Turn off heat and transfer into serving dish. Serve and enjoy.

PEA POTATO CURRY

Preparation time: 5 minutes   Cooking time: 30 minutes   Servings: 4-6

Ingredients:

1 cup green peas
3 potatoes, peeled, cut into slices
¼ teaspoon turmeric powder
2-3 garlic cloves, minced

½ teaspoon salt
¼ teaspoon black pepper
2 cups water

Directions:

Set instant pot on sauté mode.
Heat oil and fry garlic for 30-40 seconds.
Add peas and potatoes, and fry until lightly golden with few splashes of water.
Add turmeric powder, salt, black pepper, water and cover pot with lid.
Set to cook on pressure cook mode for 30 minutes.
Serve and enjoy.

SWEET POTATO CASSEROLE

Preparation time: 5 minutes   Cooking time: 40 minutes   Servings: 4

Ingredients:

4 sweet potatoes, boiled
½ teaspoon ginger powder
½ cup brown sugar
1 pinch salt

½ cup cream milk
3 eggs
4 tablespoons butter, melted

Directions:

Transfer boiled sweet potatoes, salt, milk, brown sugar, ginger powder and blend till smooth.
Crack eggs in blender and blend for another 1 minute.
Grease instant pot with butter and transfer sweet potatoes mixture, cover with lid and place to cook for 40-45 minutes on slow cook mode. Serve and enjoy.

PASTA WITH TUNA FISH

Preparation time: 5 minutes   Cooking time: 20 minutes   Servings:

Ingredients:

5 oz. tuna, water packed, drained
1 package elbow pasta, boiled
½ cup mayonnaise
½ cup sour cream
½ teaspoon salt

1 teaspoon black pepper
4 garlic cloves, minced
2 oz. cheddar cheese, shredded
2 tablespoons butter

Directions:

In instant add butter and let to melt on sauté mode. Add in tuna and stir-fry for 4-5 minutes.
Add in garlic powder, salt, pepper, mozzarella cheese, sour cream, and mayonnaise, toss to combine.
Now add pasta and cover pot with lid. Set instant pot on slow stew mode and leave to cook for 20 minutes.
Serve hot and enjoy.

Sausage Fettuccine casserole

Preparation time: 5 minutes   Cooking time: 25 minutes   Servings: 4

Ingredients:

4 oz. sausage, pieces
1 onion, chopped
¼ cup parmesan cheese, grated
¼ cup sharp cheddar cheese, grated
1 package fettuccine pasta, boiled
½ teaspoon salt

1 teaspoon black pepper
1 teaspoon garlic paste
2 tablespoons olive oil
3 tablespoons tomato ketchup
1 cup cream milk

Directions:

Heat oil in instant pot on sauté mode, add onion and sauté for 1 minute.
Add garlic with sausage and stir for 2 minutes. Season with salt and black pepper.
Pour milk and leave to simmer for 5 minutes.
Transfer boiled pasta, ketchup, parmesan cheese, cheddar cheese, stir, and cover with lid.
Let to cook for 20-25 minutes.
Serve while still hot with some fresh salad.

Chicken puffs

Preparation time: 5 minutes   Cooking time: 25 minutes   Servings: 4

Ingredients:

2 white potatoes, boiled, peeled
1 cup chicken cubes, boiled
¼ teaspoon garlic paste
¼ teaspoon salt
¼ teaspoon cumin powder

½ teaspoon chili flakes
1 onion, chopped
2 puff pastry sheets, cut into 3-4 small squares
¼ cup water

Directions:

Set instant pot on sauté mode. Heat oil and fry garlic with chicken and potatoes till lightly golden.
Season with cumin powder, salt and chili flakes. Now transfer this mixture to a bowl.
Spread puff pastry square and top with 3-4 tablespoons of chicken mixture, lift the sides of square and place over the stuffing.
Tranfer to grease instant pot and let to cook for 25 minutes on pressure cook mode.
Serve with chili garlic sauce and some salad.

DOUBLE MEATY STEW

Preparation time: 5 minutes   Cooking time: 55 minutes   Servings: 4

Ingredients:

6 oz. beef, pieces
1 chicken breast, cut into pieces
1 cup spinach, sliced
2 green chilies
1 cup tomato puree
¼ teaspoon garlic paste

1 onion, chopped
¼ teaspoon cumin powder
½ teaspoon black pepper
4 cups water
2 tablespoons cooking oil

Directions:

Set instant pot on Pressure cook mode.
Add all ingredients and place to cook for 55 minutes. Use a natural pressure release.
Serve with chili garlic sauce and enjoy.

SPICY CHICKEN FINGERS

Preparation time: 10 minutes   Cooking time: 10 minutes   Servings: 6

Ingredients:

3 chicken breasts, cut into 1 inch thick
strips
1 teaspoon garlic powder
½ cup flour
½ cup bread crumbs

½ teaspoon salt
2 eggs, whisked
½ teaspoon black pepper
½ teaspoon cinnamon powder
1 cup oil, for frying

Directions:

In a bowl combine flour, bread crumbs, salt, pepper, garlic powder, add cinnamon powder, mix well.
Dip each chicken strip into eggs then roll out in flour mixture. Place aside.
Set the instant pot on sauté mode and heat oil.
Fry each chicken finger until golden and place on paper towel. Let to drain out excess oil.
Transfer to sewing dish and serve with tomato ketchup or favorite sauce.

BAKED CHICKEN BREASTS

Preparation time: 5 minutes   Cooking time: 35 minutes   Servings: 4

Ingredients:

2 chicken breasts, skinless, boneless
2 tablespoons rice vinegar
2 tablespoons lemon juice
1 teaspoon rosemary

1 teaspoon garlic paste
1 teaspoon salt
½ teaspoon black pepper
3 tablespoons olive oil

Directions:

Combine vinegar, oil, black pepper, salt, rosemary, garlic paste, and lemon juice, in a bowl.

Drizzle over chicken and toss to combine.

Set instant pot on Pressure cooker mode and transfer chicken breasts to pot.

Leave to cook for 35 minutes. Use natural pressure release.

Serve and enjoy with a fresh salad.

Beef Fillets

Preparation time: 5 minutes   Cooking time: 60 minutes   Servings: 4

Ingredients:

2 beef fillets
1 teaspoon garlic paste
½ teaspoons ginger paste
½ teaspoon salt
½ teaspoon chili powder

½ teaspoon cinnamon powder
½ teaspoon cumin powder
2 tablespoons papaya paste
4 tablespoons oil

Directions:

In a bowl add all seasonings and mix well.

Spread on beef fillets and rub all over.

Now place fillets into the instant pot and leave to cook on pressure cook mode for 55-60 minutes.

Transfer to sewing dish and serve with any sauce.

Beef Korma

Preparation time: 5 minutes   Cooking time: 30 minutes   Servings: 4

Ingredients:

3 oz. beef, boiled
½ teaspoon garlic paste
1 teaspoon salt
2 tomatoes, chopped
½ teaspoon chili powder

¼ teaspoon turmeric powder
1 cup vegetable broth
½ teaspoon cumin powder
½ teaspoon dry coriander powder
3 tablespoons vegetable oil

Directions:

Heat oil in instant pot on sauté mode and fry garlic for 1 minute.

Add tomatoes with salt, chili powder, turmeric powder and fry.

Add in beef pieces and stir fry with few splashes of water till oil leaves the sides of the pan.

Let to simmer on low heat for 10 minutes.

Pour in vegetable broth and mix well.

Let to cook on slow cook mode for 30 minutes.

Season with cumin powder and dry coriander powder.

Serve after.

VEGETABLE PASTA

Preparation time: 5 minutes   Cooking time: 50 minutes   Servings: 4

Ingredients:

1 package pasta
½ cup peas
¼ cup cauliflower florets
1 cup asparagus, cut into 1-inch slices
1 cup basil pesto
1/4 teaspoon black pepper

2-3 garlic cloves, chopped
2 cups vegetable broth
¼ teaspoon salt
2 tablespoons cooking oil
1 12oz. package pasta

Directions:

Set instant pot on Sauté mode and heat oil. Fry garlic for 30 seconds. Add all vegetable fry for 4-5 minutes Add pasta and vegetable broth and stir well. Season with salt, basil pesto, and pepper. Leave to cook on slow cooker mode for 50 minutes. Serve while still hot.

POTATO ZUCCHINI CURRY

Preparation time: 15 minutes   Cooking time: 20 minutes   Servings: 4

Ingredients:

2 potatoes, peeled, diced
2 zucchini, sliced
¼ teaspoon chili powder
½ cup tomato puree

1 teaspoon garlic powder
2 cups vegetable broth
¼ teaspoon salt
2 tablespoons cooking oil

Directions:

Set instant pot on Sauté mode and heat oil. Fry garlic for 30 seconds.
Transfer tomatoes, chili powder, salt, and fry.
Add potatoes with zucchini and fly for 10-15 minutes.
Add pasta and vegetable broth and stir well.
Leave to cook on slow cooker mode for 20 minutes.
Serve after and enjoy.

GREEN CHICKEN CURRY

Preparation time: 5 minutes   Cooking time: 20 minutes   Servings: 4

Ingredients:

2 oz. chicken, boneless, cut into small pieces
1 bunch green coriander
2 green chilies

2-3 garlic cloves garlic, minced
1 teaspoon salt
½ teaspoon black pepper
3 tablespoons butter

Directions:

In a blender add coriander, green chili and tomatoes, blend till puree.

Melt butter in instant pot on Sauté mode and fry garlic for 1 minute.

Now add chicken and stir fly till lightly golden. Season with salt and pepper.

Add in coriander sauce and mix well.

Let to simmer for 10-15 minutes on medium heat.

Transfer to a plate and serve while still hot.

HOT TURKEY CHILI

Preparation time: 5 minutes   Cooking time: 20 minutes   Servings: 4

Ingredients:

¾ lb. turkey breasts, sliced
1 cup chili garlic sauce
¼ cup tomato ketchup
4 tablespoons honey
2 tablespoons soya sauce

2 tomatoes, chopped
¼ teaspoon salt
¼ teaspoon cayenne pepper
3 tablespoons olive oil

Directions:

Combine chili garlic sauce, tomato ketchup, soya sauce, honey, salt, pepper in a bowl.

Pour sauce on turkey and toss to combine.

Heat oil in instant pot on sauté mode and transfer turkey to instant pot.

Cover and leave to cook on pressure cook mode for 20 minutes.

Serve while still hot.

MEATY CAULIFLOWER

Preparation time: 5 minutes   Cooking time: 15 minutes   Servings: 4

Ingredients:

4 oz. beef meat, boiled
1 cup cauliflower florets
1 onion, chopped
3 garlic cloves, minced
2 tomatoes, chopped

¼ teaspoon turmeric powder
¼ teaspoon cumin powder
¼ teaspoon cinnamon powder
1 teaspoon salt
½ teaspoon chili powder

Directions:

Heat oil in instant pot on sauté mode and fry cauliflower for 3-4 minutes, place aside.

Heat a small amount of oil and fry onion for 1 minute. Add in tomatoes, chili powder, salt, and turmeric powder. Cook until fragrant.

Now add beef and stir-fry for 4 minutes. Add cauliflower and cook for 6 minutes.

Add chicken broth on and place to cook on manual mode for 10-15 minutes.

Serve while still hot, sprinkled with cinnamon and cumin.

PINEAPPLE CURRY

Preparation time: 10 minutes   Cooking time: 15 minutes   Servings: 4

Ingredients:

4 oz. beef, boiled
1 cup pineapples, chunks
½ cup pineapple juice
1 teaspoon ginger paste

½ teaspoon garlic paste
1 teaspoon salt
¼ teaspoon black pepper
3 tablespoons oil

Directions:

Heat oil in instant pot on sauté mode and cook beef with, ginger, garlic, and salt for 5-10 minutes.
Stir in pineapple chunks and toss to combine. Season with pepper. Add in pineapple juice and let to simmer for 10-15 minutes on manual mode. Serve while still hot with toasted bread.

INSTANT FISH FINGERS

Preparation time: 5 minutes   Cooking time: 10 minutes   Servings: 4

Ingredients:

2 white fish fillets, cut into strips
1 teaspoon salt
1 teaspoon black pepper
1 teaspoon garlic powder

3 tablespoons almond flour
1 teaspoon rosemary
Oil for frying

Directions:

In a bowl add all seasoning and mix well.
Add in fish fingers and toss to coat well.
Now heat oil in instant pot and fry fish pieces until nicely golden.
Serve with fresh salad.

TAMARIND TUNA

Preparation time: 5 minutes   Cooking time: 15 minutes   Servings: 4

Ingredients:

4 tuna fish fillets
2 tablespoons extra-virgin olive oil
1 teaspoon fine sea salt
1 teaspoon black pepper

Lemon wedges, for serving
2 tablespoons lemon juice
1 teaspoon tamarind paste

Directions:

Sprinkle salt and pepper on fish. Drizzle lemon juice, tamarind paste, and oil all over fish.
Place it into greased instant pot and let to cook for 15 minutes on the pressure cooker. Release pressure naturally. Serve with lemon wedges.

*F*ISH PATTIES

Preparation time: 10 minutes   Cooking time: 10 minutes   Servings: 4

Ingredients:

2 fish fillets, cut into pieces
1 teaspoon salt
1 teaspoon black pepper
1 tablespoon coriander, chopped

¼ teaspoon garlic paste
4 tablespoons almond flour
1 potato, boiled
½ cup oil for frying

Directions:

Fry fish till lightly golden in a skillet or instant pot on Saute function.

Now crumble with folk and place aside.

Combine fish, potatoes, garlic, coriander, salt, and pepper and mix well.

Make small round patties with this mixture and place into the platter.

Heat oil in instant pot and shallow fry patties on sauté mode until lightly golden.

Serve with salad or hot sauce.

*C*HICKEN TURNIP STEW

Preparation time: 10 minutes   Cooking time: 30 minutes   Servings: 6

Ingredients:

1 onion, chopped
2 tomatoes, chopped
1 cup chicken pieces
2-3 turnips, peeled, diced
2 cups chicken broth
1 carrot, sliced
1 tablespoon coriander, chopped
½ teaspoon garlic paste

½ teaspoon minced ginger
½ teaspoon cumin powder
½ teaspoon cinnamon powder
½ teaspoon chili powder
¼ teaspoon salt
¼ teaspoon turmeric powder
3 tablespoons oil
2 green chilies, whole

Directions:

Heat oil in instant pot, sauté onion for 1 minute on Sauté mode.

Stir in tomatoes, ginger garlic paste, salt, chili powder, turmeric powder and cook for 1 minute.

Add chicken pieces, and cook until golden.

Add turnip and cook until tender.

Now add chicken broth, coriander, carrot, green chili, and leave to cook on low heat for 30 minutes on Stew mode.

Add cinnamon and cumin powder and stir.

Serve while still hot with fresh bread.

BEEF AND OKRA

Preparation time: 5 minutes   Cooking time: 30 minutes   Servings: 4

Ingredients:

2 oz. beef, boiled, sliced
1 cup okra, sliced
1 tomato, chopped
1 onion, sliced
1 teaspoon garlic paste

¼ teaspoon ginger paste
¼ teaspoon turmeric powder
¼ teaspoon salt
¼ teaspoon chili powder
3 cups chicken broth

Directions:

Heat oil in instant pot on sauté mod and fry okra till nicely golden on Sauté mode. Transfer to platter and place aside.

In the same pot add onion and cook for 5 minutes. Stir in garlic, ginger, tomatoes, salt, chili powder, turmeric powder and cook for 6 minutes.

Add beef and cook for 5-6 minutes. Now add fried okra and stir cook for 10-15 minutes.

Sprinkle cumin powder and cinnamon powder.

Serve while still hot.

LAMB MUSHROOM CURRY

Preparation time: 10 minutes   Cooking time: 15 minutes   Servings: 4

Ingredients:

4 oz. lamb, boiled
1 cup mushrooms, sliced
1 onion, chopped
2 garlic cloves, minced
2 tomatoes, chopped
1 carrot, chopped
¼ teaspoon turmeric powder

¼ teaspoon cumin powder
¼ teaspoon cinnamon powder
1 teaspoon salt
½ teaspoon chili powder
4 tablespoons olive oil
½ cup chicken broth
1 green chili

Directions:

Heat oil in instant pot and cook onion for 1 minute.

Add in tomatoes, chili powder, salt, turmeric powder, and fry.

Now add mutton and cook for 5 minutes. Add the carrot, mushrooms and cook for 5 minutes.

Add chicken broth on and place to cook on manual Mode for 10-15 minutes. Release steam naturally.

Serve sprinkled with cumin and cinnamon.

SLOW COOKED PORK AND ZUCCHINIS

Preparation time: 5 minutes   Cooking time: 60 minutes   Servings: 4

Ingredients:

10oz. pork, sliced
2 zucchini, sliced
3 turnips, peeled, diced
1 onion, chopped
4 garlic cloves, minced

2 tomatoes, chopped
¼ teaspoon turmeric powder
1 teaspoon salt
½ teaspoon chili powder
4 tablespoons olive oil

Directions:

In instant, pot add all ingredients and toss to combine. Let to cook for 60 minutes on slow cook mode. Serve while still hot.

BEEF AND PUMPKIN

Preparation time: 5 minutes   Cooking time: 60 minutes   Servings: 4

Ingredients:

¾ lb. beef, cut into small cubes
2 turnips, peeled, diced
2 cups pumpkin, cubed
1 onion, sliced

2 garlic cloves, minced
1 teaspoon salt
½ teaspoon chili powder
4 tablespoons olive oil

Directions:

In instant, pot add all ingredients and toss to combine. Let to cook for 60 minutes on slow cook mode. Serve while still hot with fresh bread.

INSTANT CREAMY TILAPIA

Preparation time: minutes   Cooking time: 20 minutes   Servings: 4

Ingredients:

4 4 oz. tilapia fillets
2 tablespoons lemon juice
2 tablespoons of lemon juice
½ teaspoon of black pepper

2 tablespoons chopped fresh dill weed
½ teaspoon salt
Cooking spray

Directions:

Grease instant pot with cooking spray and place fish filets sprinkle salt, and dill.
Drizzle lemon juice and toss to combine. Let to roast for 20 minutes on Pressure cook mode.
Add cream cheese, black pepper, and toss to combine.
Simmer for 2 minutes.
Serve and enjoy.

SAUSAGE AND PEPPERS IN SAUCE

Preparation time: 5 minutes   Cooking time: 10 minutes   Servings: 6

Ingredients:

2 tbsp. extra-virgin olive oil
2 lb. Italian sausage
2 bell peppers, diced
2 zucchini chopped
1 chopped onion

1 (28 oz.) can Italian tomatoes
1 (16 oz.) can Arrabiata pasta sauce
½ lb. penne pasta
1 ½ tablespoons Italian seasoning
Grated parmesan cheese

Directions:

Select brown mode, take away the sausage meat from the casing and place them within the instant with olive oil and cook until crumbled and browned.

Drain the fat away and add all the remaining ingredients except cheese, stirring for 3 minutes.

Lock the lid of the instant pot and cook for 8-10 minutes. Do a quick pressure release and unlock.

Garnish with parmesan cheese and serve immediately.

PORK STROGANOFF AND SPAGHETTI

Preparation time: 5 minutes   Cooking time: 30 minutes   Servings: 6

Ingredients:

2 lb. pork sirloin tip roast
1 tablespoon olive oil
1 medium onion, chopped
1 cup dry white wine
1 tablespoon Dijon mustard
1 cup low sodium chicken broth
1 tablespoon all-purpose flour

1lb. button mushrooms
3 carrots
2 stalks celery
¼ cup Neufchatel cheese
¼ cup roughly chopped fresh parsley
12 oz. spaghetti
Salt and pepper, to taste

Directions:

Season the pork generously with salt and pepper.

Heat oil in the instant pot, select Brown mode and add pork. Cook until browned.

Add the onions, cook for 5 minutes.

Add dry white wine, mustard, and flour. Bring this to simmer and cook till reduced half.

Add the chicken broth, celery, carrots, and mushrooms.

Select manual mode and close the lid and bring to high pressure over medium heat and cook for 18 minutes. Release the pressure by using quick release method.

Stir in the cheese, parsley and adjust seasonings. Place aside for 5 minutes. Cook spaghettis until al dente. Stir spaghettis in prepared stroganoff.

Serve after.

Braised pork with Marinara sauce

Preparation time: 5 minutes   Cooking time: 30 minutes   Servings: 6

Ingredients:

3lb. pork loin roast
2 tablespoons olive oil
1 tablespoons Italian seasoning

1 cup Marinara sauce
Salt and pepper, to taste

Directions:

Rub the pork with salt, pepper, and Italian seasoning.

Select brown mode, heat the olive oil and add the pork, cook until evenly browned.

Pour 1 ½ cup water and shut the lid. Select manual mode and cook for 25 minutes on high pressure.

Do a natural pressure release and then open the lid slowly.

Add the marinara sauce and let the pork coat the sauce well.

Place the pork to rest for 5 minutes before slicing.

Serve while still hot with marinara sauce.

Tuna pasta salad

Preparation time: 5 minutes   Cooking time: 15 minutes   Servings: 6

Ingredients:

1 tablespoon olive oil
3 anchovies
1 garlic clove, minced
Salt, to taste
2 cups tomato puree
16-oz. dried fusilli pasta, cooked

11oz. olive oil packed tuna, divided
Water, as required
1 cup tomato, chopped
2 tablespoons capers, rinsed
6 cups lettuce leaves, torn into pieces

Directions:

Select the Sauté setting of an instant pot and heat the oil.

Add anchovies and garlic and sauté for about 1 minute.

Add salt, tomato puree, pasta and half the tuna and stir to combine. Pour enough water to cover the mixture. Lock the instant pot.

Select the Manual setting and cook for 3 minutes. Unplug the pot and wait for at least 10 minutes.

By using the natural release method, release the pressure.

Carefully, uncover the instant pot and immediately, stir in remaining tuna.

Transfer the mixture into a large bowl and let it cool.

Add remaining ingredients and stir to combine.

Serve immediately.

WHITE WINE SALMON

Preparation time: 5 minutes   Cooking time: 6 minutes   Servings: 4

Ingredients:

4 (6 oz.) salmon steaks
½ cup white wine
1 tablespoons low sodium soy sauce

2 tablespoons maple syrup
2 tablespoons balsamic vinegar
½ teaspoon lemon pepper seasoning

Directions:

Rinse the salmon and at them dry with towels.

Select Steam and add all the other ingredients along with the salmon steaks in the instant pot.

Lock the lid and set the timer to cook for 6 minutes.

Remove the cooked salmon steaks, and simmer remaining sauce until thicken.

Serve steaks with sauce.

STEAMED CLAMS AND CHEESE

Preparation time: 5 minutes   Cooking time: 3 minutes   Servings: 6

Ingredients:

2 lb. shell clams
1/2 cup white wine
1 stick butter
2 teaspoon garlic powder

½ cup grated cheese, Parmesan or
Cheddar
2/3 cup fresh lemon juice

Directions:

Mix lemon juice, white wine and butter in a microwave for a minute on high.

Stir the mixture and chill for a day.

On your instant pot, Select steam mode.

Place a rack in the instant pot and pour white wine and lemon juice mixture.

Place the clams onto the rack. Lock the lid and high pressure for 3 minutes. Use a quick pressure release method and open the pot.

Serve clams with toasted bread.

SHRIMP MAC AND CHEESE

Preparation time: 5 minutes   Cooking time: 6 minutes   Servings: 6

Ingredients:

16 oz. elbow macaroni
1 tablespoon olive oil
8 oz. ricotta cheese
1 cup shrimps, crumbs coated and deep fried

1 sprig parsley or basil, finely chopped
½ cup pecorino Romano, grated
Salt and pepper, to taste

Directions:

In the Instant pot, add oil, pasta, salt and enough water to cover the pasta.

Select manual mode and cover the lid and cook this on high pressure for 4-6 minutes.

Do a quick pressure release and unlock the lid carefully.

Open and mix parsley, ricotta cheese and evenly distribute shrimps.

Serve and top with grated cheese.

KIELBASA IN COCONUT MILK

Preparation time: 5 minutes   Cooking time: 10 minutes   Servings: 4

Ingredients:

2 tbsp. butter
1 large onion, chopped
2 stalks celery, chopped
4 large carrots, peeled and diced
4 medium potatoes, diced
1 lb. kielbasa, sliced
2 cups fish stock

1 cup chilly water
1 bay leaf
½ teaspoon dried thyme
1 cup coconut milk
1 cup thawed corn kernels
Salt and pepper, to taste

Directions:

Heat butter in the instant pot and sauté onions for 3 minutes.

Stir in the remaining ingredients except for corn, and coconut milk.

Select manual mode and lock the instant pot lid and cook for 5 minutes.

Unlock and add coconut milk, and corn. Simmer for 10 minutes.

Serve while still hot.

BEEF AND RAVIOLI IN SAUCE

Preparation time: 5 minutes   Cooking time: 12 minutes   Servings: 4

Ingredients:

1lb. ground beef
1 large bag frozen ravioli
1 jar spaghetti sauce

Water, as required
Salt and pepper, to taste

Directions:

Select the Sauté setting off instant pot.

Add beef and sauté for about 6- 8 minutes. Drain the fat from pot.

Add ravioli and spaghetti sauce and stir to combine.

Add enough water to cover the mixture.

Close the instant pot by locking the lid.

Select the Manual setting on low pressure and cook for about 3 minutes.

By using the quick release method, release the pressure. Serve while still hot.

PASTA WITH SQUID AND SHRIMPS

Preparation time: 5 minutes   Cooking time: 10 minutes   Servings: 6

Ingredients:

8 oz. cooked fettuccine, drained
1 ½ lb. uncooked squid, cut into rounds
½ lb. shrimps
1 cup onion, chopped
1 cup seafood stock
½ lb. scallops
½ cup white wine

1/3 cup soy sauce
¼ cup hoisin sauce
1 tablespoon minced garlic
2 tablespoons lemon juice
2 tablespoons butter
1/3 cup grated parmesan cheese
Salt and pepper, to taste

Directions:

Rinse the shrimps and scallops under cold water and pat dry them.

Select sauté and heat butter in the instant pot, add onions and garlic, cook until soft and tender.

Add all the ingredients including the seafood and stir well.

Select manual mode and lock the lid and cook on high pressure for 5 minutes.

Do a natural pressure release and spoon the seafood mixture on the cooked pasta.

Garnish with grated parmesan cheese.

Appetizers and side dishes

Mozzarella Sticks

Preparation time: 5 minutes   Cooking time: 10 minutes   Servings: 6

Ingredients:

6 oz. mozzarella cheese, cut into 1-inch strips
1 teaspoon onion powder
1 cup bread crumbs
1 egg, whisked

1 teaspoon garlic powder
½ teaspoon salt
½ teaspoon chili powder
½ teaspoon cinnamon powder
1 cup oil, for frying

Directions:

In a bowl, combine bread crumbs, onion powder, salt, chili powder, garlic, cumin powder, and toss.
Dip each mozzarella stick into egg then roll out into bread crumbs mixture.
Heat oil in instant pot on sauté mode. Transfer sticks into oil and fry till nicely golden.
Place on paper towel. Let to drain out excess oil.
Transfer to sewing dish and serve with any sauce.
Enjoy.

Classic Potato Chips

Preparation time: 5 minutes   Cooking time: 10 minutes   Servings: 4

Ingredients:

4 potatoes, sliced thinly
¼ teaspoon salt
1 teaspoon thyme
¼ teaspoon black pepper

¼ garlic powder
2 tablespoons lemon juice
½ cup cooking oil, for frying

Directions:

Heat oil in instant pot on sauté mode.
Fry some chips till nicely golden and crispy.
Transfer to paper towel and let to drain out excess oil.
Season with thyme, garlic powder, salt, and pepper.
Drizzle lemon juice and enjoy.

*I*NSTANT MUSHROOMS

Preparation time: 5 minutes   Cooking time: 15 minutes   Servings: 4

Ingredients:

4oz. mushrooms, sliced
¼ teaspoon salt
¼ teaspoon black pepper

¼ garlic powder
4 tablespoons oil, for frying

Directions:

Heat oil in instant pot on sauté mode.
Fry mushrooms till nicely golden.
Transfer to paper towel and let to drain out excess oil.
Season with garlic powder, salt, and pepper.
Serve and enjoy.

*F*RIED SHRIMPS

Preparation time: 5 minutes   Cooking time: 10 minutes   Servings: 2

Ingredients:

6oz. shrimps, peeled, deveined
¼ teaspoon salt
¼ teaspoon black pepper

2 tablespoons lemon juice
1 teaspoon garlic powder
2 tablespoons oil, for frying

Directions:

Heat oil in instant pot on sauté mode.
Add shrimps and cook for 5 minutes.
Season with salt, garlic, and pepper. Fry for another 5 minutes.
Serve while still hot with lemon juice.

*M*ASHED RICE AND POTATOES

Preparation time: 5 minutes   Cooking time: 55 minutes   Servings: 4

Ingredients:

1 cup rice, soaked
2 potatoes, peeled, diced
1 pinch salt
¼ teaspoon black pepper

2 cups of water
2 tablespoons olive oil
1 onion, chopped
2 garlic cloves, minced

Directions:

Transfer all ingredients into an instant pot and set it to slow cook mode.
Let to cook for 55 minutes. Let the ingredients cool and then mash with potato masher.
Serve after.

CRISPY OKRA

Preparation time: 5 minutes   Cooking time: 10 minutes   Servings: 4

Ingredients:

6 oz. okra, heads removed
½ teaspoon salt

½ teaspoon black pepper
¼ cup oil, for frying

Directions:

Slice the okra lengthwise. Heat oil in instant pot on sauté mode. Transfer okra into oil and fry until golden. Place on paper towel. Let to drain out excess oil. Season with salt and pepper. Serve after.

SPICY CARROTS

Preparation time: 15 minutes   Cooking time: 35 minutes   Servings: 4

Ingredients:

4 large carrots, sliced
¼ teaspoon salt
¼ teaspoon black pepper

2 tablespoons lemon juice
1 cup orange juice
2 tablespoons oil, for frying

Directions:

Heat oil in instant pot on sauté mode.
Add carrots and let to simmer for 10-15 minutes.
Season with salt and pepper. Add in orange juice.
Cover and leave to cook on slow cook mode for 35 minutes.
Drizzle lemon juice on top before serving.

POTATO WEDGES

Preparation time: 5 minutes   Cooking time: 15 minutes   Servings: 4

Ingredients:

4 large potatoes, cut into wings
2 tablespoons gram flour
1 teaspoon garlic powder
½ teaspoon salt
½ teaspoon black pepper

½ teaspoon cinnamon powder
½ teaspoon cumin powder
2 tablespoons lemon juice
1 cup oil, for frying

Directions:

In a bowl, combine flour, salt, garlic, pepper, cumin powder, cinnamon powder, and toss.
Add in potato wings and toss to combine.
Heat oil in instant pot on sauté mode. Transfer potatoes into oil and fry till nicely golden.
Place on paper towel. Let to drain out excess oil. Transfer to a serving dish, drizzle lemon juice on top and serve.

GARLIC BREAD

Preparation time: 5 minutes   Cooking time: 15 minutes   Servings: 4

Ingredients:

1 French baguette, sliced
3 garlic cloves, minced
2 tablespoons oil

½ teaspoon salt
½ teaspoon black pepper

Directions:

With the help of a sharp knife, cut baguette to make 8 slices.

Mix olive oil, garlic, black pepper, and salt in a bowl.

Brush this mixture onto each bread slice and transfer to baking sheet.

Now put this sheet into the instant pot and let it cook for 15 minutes on pressure cook mode.

Serve after as a side dish for beef soup or appetizer.

CHICKEN FRITTERS

Preparation time: 5 minutes   Cooking time: 20 minutes   Servings: 6

Ingredients:

6 chicken breast's fillets
½ cup bread crumbs
1 teaspoon garlic powder
1 teaspoon onion powder
1 teaspoon dry coriander powder

1 teaspoon cumin powder
2 eggs
1 teaspoon salt
1/2 teaspoon black pepper

Directions:

In a bowl mix breadcrumbs with coriander powder, onion powder, cumin powder, salt, black pepper and toss well. Whisk the eggs in a bowl. Dip the chicken into eggs.

Roll each chicken fillet into breadcrumb's mixture and transfer into the platter.

Place chicken fillets into the instant pot and set it on pressure cook mode. Cook for 20 minutes.

Serve while still hot with sauce.

FRIED CAULIFLOWER

Preparation time: 5 minutes   Cooking time: 10 minutes   Servings: 4

Ingredients:

1 cup cauliflower florets
1 teaspoon onion powder
1 cup all-purpose flour
1 teaspoon garlic powder
½ teaspoon salt

½ teaspoon chili powder
½ teaspoon cinnamon powder
1 cup oil, for frying

Directions:

In a bowl combine flour, onion powder, salt, chili powder, garlic, cumin powder, and toss.
Add in cauliflower and mix well.
Heat oil in instant pot on sauté mode. Transfer cauliflower into oil and fry until golden.
Place on paper towel. Let to drain out excess oil.
Transfer to sewing dish and serve with any sauce.

Mashed Potatoes

Preparation time: 5 minutes   Cooking time: 30 minutes   Servings: 4

Ingredients:

4 potatoes, peeled   1 pinch salt
1 cup sour cream   ¼ teaspoon black pepper
½ cup heavy cream

Directions:

Place the potatoes, sour cream, and heavy cream into an instant pot and cover with lid.
Leave to cook on slow cook mode for 30 minutes.
Season with salt and pepper.
Serve and enjoy.

Rice and Carrots

Preparation time: 5 minutes   Cooking time: 8 minutes   Servings: 2

Ingredients:

1 cup white rice   1 carrot, shredded
1 ½ cups water

Directions:

Place the ingredients in the instant pot.
Set to high pressure and cook for 8 minutes.
Allow pressure to release naturally.

Beans Side Dish

Preparation time: 5 minutes   Cooking time: 10 minutes   Servings: 2

Ingredients:

1 cup kidney beans, soaked and rinsed   1 ½ cups beef broth

Directions:

Place the ingredients in the instant pot. Set to high pressure and cook for 8 minutes.
Release pressure naturally and serve.

MILLET AND GARLIC

Preparation time: 5 minutes   Cooking time: 10 minutes   Servings: 2

Ingredients:

1 cup millet
1 ½ cups water

1 tablespoon garlic powder

Directions:

Place the ingredients in the instant pot. Set to high pressure and cook for 8 minutes.
Allow pressure to release naturally. Serve while still hot.

BROCCOLI BULGUR

Preparation time: 5 minutes   Cooking time: 10 minutes   Servings: 4

Ingredients:

1 cup bulgur
1 ½ cups vegetable stock

½ cup broccoli florets

Directions:

Place the ingredients in the instant pot.
Set to high pressure and cook for 8 minutes.
Allow pressure to release naturally. Serve after.

QUINOA AND KALE

Preparation time: 5 minutes   Cooking time: 10 minutes   Servings: 4

Ingredients:

1 cup quinoa
1 ½ cups water

1 cup chopped kale
1 teaspoon garlic salt

Directions:

Place the ingredients in the instant pot. Set to high pressure and cook for 8 minutes.
Allow pressure to release naturally. Serve after.

DELUXE POTATOES

Preparation time: 5 minutes   Cooking time: 25 minutes   Servings: 4

Ingredients:

1 teaspoon pepper
1 teaspoon garlic powder
1 cup broccoli florets

2 cups cheese, cheddar
2 tablespoons butter, melted
5 potatoes

Directions:

Take the potatoes and poke them with a fork. After melting the butter, dip them in butter and then wrap each of them in some tin foil.

Place these potatoes in the pressure cooker and place the lid on top. Cook this at a high setting for 20 minutes. When done, take the potatoes out of the instant pot and allow them a minute to cool down. Then slice up the potatoes in half.

Stuff these with the broccoli and cheddar cheese and then sprinkle with some garlic and pepper. Wrap back up in the tin foil and place in the instant pot.

Let them warm up for a few minutes so that the cheese can begin to melt.

Serve potatoes with a fish or meat dish.

PARSNIP GRATIN

Preparation time: 5 minutes   Cooking time: 10 minutes   Servings: 4

Ingredients:

2 cups mozzarella cheese
1 cup cream cheese
1 tablespoon garlic powder
1 tablespoon pepper
2 cups vegetable broth

3 cloves garlic, chopped
2 cups sliced parsnips
3 tablespoons olive oil
Salt and pepper, to taste

Directions:

Place all ingredients in instant pot, except the cheese. Lock the lid and cook on high pressure for 4 minutes. Allow the pressure to come out on its own. After the pressure is gone, add in the mozzarella cheese.

Set the instant pot to Saute and cook for 5 minutes.

Serve after.

STEAMED ARTICHOKES

Preparation time: 5 minutes   Cooking time: 10 minutes   Servings: 4

Ingredients:

2 medium artichokes
1 cup of water
1 lemon cut in half

2 tablespoons of mayonnaise
1 teaspoon of Dijon mustard
1 pinch of paprika

Directions:

Clean, trim and wash the artichokes. Place the steamer rack in your instant pot and then pour in the water. Place the artichokes on the rack facing upwards. Drizzle with lemon juice.

Close the lid of the instant pot and lock. Then, you will cook the artichokes for 10 minutes on high pressure. After the cooking process is complete, use the natural release process in order to release the pressure from your instant pot.

Meanwhile, mix the mayonnaise, mustard, and paprika. Serve artichokes with prepared dip.

ROSEMARY POTATOES

Preparation time: 5 minutes   Cooking time: 15 minutes   Servings: 4

Ingredients:

10-12 baby potatoes   2 sprigs fresh rosemary
1 ½ cups water   2 tablespoons herb butter

Directions:

Place water and rosemary in the pot and place the rack or metal trivet. Wash and keep the baby potatoes on the steamer rack. Spin and lock the lid. Select pressure cook and adjust to high pressure for 8-10 minutes.
Do a pressure release and remove the baby potatoes carefully.
Rub the potatoes with herb butter and grill in the oven for 5- 6 minutes to get the crispy golden skin.
Serve after.

STEAMED CORN

Preparation time: 5 minutes   Cooking time: 5 minutes   Servings: 4

Ingredients:

1 cup corn kernels   ½ tablespoon lemon juice
1 ½ cups water   Butter, to rub the corn kernels
Salt and pepper

Directions:

Place water in the instant pot and place the rack or metal trivet.
Wash and keep corn kernels on the steamer rack.
Spin and lock the lid, select manual button and cook this on high-pressure 5-6 minutes.
Do a pressure release and remove the corn kernels carefully.
Mix the steamed corn kernels with salt and pepper, lemon juice and butter.

ZUCCHINI CHIPS

Preparation time: 5 minutes   Cooking time: 10 minutes   Servings: 6

Ingredients:

3 large zucchinis, thinly sliced   ¼ teaspoon black pepper
¼ teaspoon salt   ½ tablespoons cooking oil, for frying

Directions:

Heat oil in instant pot on sauté mode. Transfer few slices of instant pot and fry until nicely golden and crispy.
Repeat same steps for all zucchini chips.
Tranfer to paper towel and let to drain out excess oil. Season with salt and pepper.
Serve and enjoy.

ROASTED FENNEL AND TOMATOES

Preparation time: 5 minutes   Cooking time: 30 minutes   Servings: 4

Ingredients:

4 fennel bulbs, timed and quartered
4 cherry tomatoes
1 pinch caraway seeds
1 tablespoon olive oil

¼ teaspoon salt
¼ teaspoon red chili flakes
2 cups vegetable broth

Directions:

Place funnel bulbs into instant pot with tomatoes and olive oil.
Add all remaining ingredients. Cook on slow cook mode until fennels are tender.
Serve and enjoy.

THYME POTATO MASH

Preparation time: 5 minutes   Cooking time: 25 minutes   Servings: 4

Ingredients:

4 potatoes
1 teaspoon salt
1 teaspoon black pepper

1 teaspoon garlic paste/powder
4 tablespoons olive oil
3 sprigs of fresh thyme

Directions:

Peel and wash potatoes.
Prick potatoes a bit with folk. Drizzle few drops of oil on potatoes and place to instant pot let to cook them for 20-25 minutes on pressure cook mode. Put them in a large bowl and add all remaining ingredients. Mash with the potato masher. Sprinkle black paper on top and serve.

CHICKPEA HUMMUS

Preparation time: 5 minutes   Cooking time: 55 minutes   Servings: 6

Ingredients:

1 cup chickpea, soaked
1 pinch salt
¼ teaspoon chili powder

3 cups of water
2 tablespoons olive oil
2 garlic cloves, minced

Directions:

Transfer water, chickpea, salt, and garlic into the instant pot. Set it on pressure cook mode.
Cover with lid and leave to cook for 55 minutes.
Now let to cool a little then transfer boiled chickpea into a blender and blend until smooth.
Add olive oil gradually and blend.
Transfer to a serving dish and sprinkle with chili powder.

*S*OY SAUCE SPINACH

Preparation time: 5 minutes   Cooking time: 10 minutes   Servings: 2

Ingredients:

1 bunch baby spinach leaves
½ teaspoon salt
1 teaspoon black pepper
2 garlic cloves, minced

1 tablespoon soy sauce
1 teaspoon lemon juice
2 tablespoons oil

Directions:

Heat oil in instant pot and stir fry garlic for 1 minute on sauté mode.
Add spinach and sauté for 10-15 minutes.
Season it with salt, pepper, soy sauce, and lemon juice.
Serve and enjoy.

*C*ARAMELIZED ONIONS

Preparation time: 5 minutes   Cooking time: 10 minutes   Servings: 6

Ingredients:

3 large onion bulbs
1 cup water

1 teaspoon sugar
Salt and pepper, to taste

Directions:

Slice off 1/4th of the onion bulb from the top keeping the bulb intact.
Prepare the Instant pot by adding water and place the rack on it.
Keep the onion bulb on the rack and select pressure cook for 5-6 minutes on high pressure.
Do a natural pressure release and remove the soft onion very carefully.
Select brown option on the pot and place the onion inside for 5 minutes with sugar, until crisp and brown.
Serve with beef meals.

TOMATOES AND CHEESE

Preparation time: 5 minutes   Cooking time: 10 minutes   Servings: 6

Ingredients:

3 large tomatoes
1 cup water

3 teaspoons herb butter
1 cup shredded mozzarella cheese

Directions:

Slice off 1/4th of the tomato bulb from the top keeping the bulb intact.

Prepare the pot by adding water and place the rack on it.

Scoop out the inner filling of the tomato and place the tomato on the rack. Select pressure cook for 5-6 minutes on high pressure.

Do a natural pressure release and remove the soft steamed tomato very carefully. Stuff the tomato with herb butter and mozzarella cheese.

Broil the tomatoes in the oven for 5 minutes to get crispy skin.

Serve with chicken dishes.

POLENTA WITH CHILI FLAKES

Preparation time: 5 minutes   Cooking time: 8 minutes   Servings: 4-6

Ingredients:

2 cups coarse polenta
8 cups liquid

2 teaspoons salt
2 tablespoons red paprika flakes

Directions:

Fill the pot with water and bring it to a boil.

Add salt and polenta flour to the boiling water.

Keep stirring this continuously and close the lid of the pot.

Select Manual program on the Instant pot and cook this on high pressure for 8 minutes.

Do a natural pressure release and check for the doneness of polenta.

Serve while still hot with pork.

Desserts

RICE PUDDING WITH APRICOTS

Preparation time: 5 minutes   Cooking time: 60 minutes   Servings: 4

Ingredients:

6 apricots, chopped
1 cup pineapple chunks
1 cup rice
½ cup sugar
1 cup raisins

2 green cardamoms
1oz. pistachios, chopped
2 cups milk
1 cup water
1 pinch salt

Directions:

In instant pot transfer rice, apricots, pineapple, sugar, milk, salt, and cardamom, cover with lid.

Let it cook on slow cook mode for 60 minutes.

Place pudding into the freezer for 15 minutes and top with pistachios before serving.

RASPBERRY CAKE

Preparation time: 5 minutes   Cooking time: 40 minutes   Servings: 4

Ingredients:

2 cups all-purpose flour
1 cup fresh raspberries
2 cups strawberry puree
1 teaspoon baking powder
1 cup butter
1 pinch salt

2 eggs
1 cup milk
1 cup sugar
1 cup whipped cream
2 tablespoons caster sugar
1 teaspoon vanilla extract

Directions:

In instant pot place a trivet and add 2-3 cups water in a pot.

In a bowl, add flour, eggs, sugar, salt, baking powder, milk, butter, vanilla extract and beat well.

Add strawberry puree and stir. Pour into greased cake pan and place on a trivet. Top with fresh raspberries.

Lock the lid and cook for 40 minutes on pressure cook mode.

Toss caster sugar with whipped cream to combine.

When the cake is cooled top it with whipped cream.

LEMON APPLE CAKE

Preparation time: 5 minutes   Cooking time: 40 minutes   Servings: 6

Ingredients:

2 cups all-purpose flour
2 tablespoons lemon zest
2 tablespoons lemon juice
1 teaspoon baking powder
¼ teaspoon baking soda
½ cup butter

1 pinch salt
4 eggs
1 cup coconut milk
1 cup sugar
½ cup honey
½ cup apple jam

Directions:

In instant pot place stand or trivet, add 2 cups of water.

Combine flour, sugar, salt, baking powder, baking soda, eggs, lemon juice butter, milk, 1 tablespoon lemon zest and beat with an electric whisk.

Transfer to grease baking pan and place on a trivet, cover, and leave to cook on pressure cook mode for 30-40 minutes.

Combine apple jam with honey. Pour this mixture over cake and top with lemon zest.

Serve after.

CHOCOLATE COOKIES

Preparation time: 10 minutes   Cooking time: 10 minutes   Servings: 12 cookies

Ingredients:

1 cups all-purpose flour
1 cup cocoa powder
1/2 cup molten chocolate
1/2 teaspoon baking powder

1/2 cup butter
2 eggs
1 cup caster sugar

Directions:

Grease instant pot with cooking spray.

Combine all ingredients in a bowl and knead a soft dough.

Roll out dough on a clean surface and cut with cookie cutter.

Place into greased instant pot and let to prepare for 8 minutes on manual mode on high.

Serve at room temperature.

MAPLE BREAD PUDDING

Preparation time: 5 minutes   Cooking time: 12 minutes   Servings: 8

Ingredients:

1 cup melted butter

8 slices bread

1 cup maple syrup

4 eggs

1 cup whipping cream

1 teaspoon vanilla extract

Directions:

Grease an oven safe form that fits in your instant pot with the butter

Combine the syrup, eggs, cream, and vanilla.

Place the bread in the instant pot and pour the cream mixture over it. Cover with tin foil.

Set instant pot to high pressure and adjust the valve to manual.

Cook for 12 minutes and allow pressure to release on its own.

Serve with vanilla ice cream.

COCONUT NECTAR RICE PUDDING

Preparation time: 5 minutes   Cooking time: 6 hours   Servings: 4

Ingredients:

1 cup melted butter

1cup heavy cream

1 1/2 cups water

1 teaspoon almond extract

1 cup maple syrup

1 cup instant rice

2 eggs

½ teaspoon vanilla extract

2 tablespoons coconut nectar

Directions:

Grease an oven safe form that fits in your instant pot with the butter.

Combine all ingredients together in a baking dish.

Slow cook for 6 hours.

Serve after.

PEANUT BUTTER CHOCOLATE PUDDING

Preparation time: 5 minutes   Cooking time: 15 minutes   Servings: 4

Ingredients:

1 tablespoon cornstarch

2 tablespoon peanut butter

3 tablespoons cocoa powder

2 cups whipping cream

4 eggs

3 cups maple syrup

1 cup butter, melted

Directions:

Fill up the baking pan with ingredients. Mix well.

Pour 2 cups water in instant pot and insert trivet. Place the baking dish onto trivet and lock the lid.

Cook on to a steam function for 15 minutes.

Serve this warm or leave in the fridge so that it can cool down first before enjoying.

PEAR CHEESECAKE

Preparation time: 5 minutes   Cooking time: 10 minutes   Servings: 8

Ingredients:

1 teaspoon vanilla
3 eggs

4 cups cream cheese
½ cup pear sauce

Directions:

Take out your pie pan and make sure that it fits in the instant pot.

Grease this pan up with some coconut oil or butter.

Take out a bowl and mix together the eggs, cream cheese, vanilla, and applesauce. Wien this is well combined, you can place the ingredients in the pie pan.

Place the lid on the instant pot and turn it on a high setting. Cook for 10 minutes.

Use the natural release pressure to let out the steam. Once it is done, take the lid off.

Allow the cheesecake some time to cool down before serving.

CHOCOLATE ZUCCHINI BREAD

Preparation time: 5 minutes   Cooking time: 18 minutes   Servings: 6

Ingredients:

1 teaspoon baking powder
½ cup heavy cream
2 eggs
1 cup applesauce
2 shredded zucchinis

2 cups flour
2 cups brown sugar
½ cup chocolate chips
1 cup melted butter

Directions:

Take out a bowl and mix together all the ingredients. Pick out a bread pan that will fit into the instant pot and then grease it up with butter.

Pour the batter into the pan and cover everything with some tin foil.

Add the bread pan and some water to the instant pot and then put the lid on top.

Cook this on a high pressure for about 18 minutes. Allow a few minutes for the pressure to naturally escape. Serve warm with chocolate spread.

PEARS AND DATES

Preparation time: 5 minutes   Cooking time: 20 minutes   Servings: 4

Ingredients:

1 tablespoons maple syrup
1 cup water
1 teaspoon vanilla

1 cup dates, chopped
3 cup pears, peeled and chopped

Directions:

Place all ingredients in instant pot.

Stir well and select Low pressure. Cook for 20 minutes.

Use a natural pressure release method.

Serve with vanilla ice cream.

CHOCOLATE PUDDING

Preparation time: 10 minutes   Cooking time: 10 minutes   Servings: 4

Ingredients:

1 cup dark chocolate, melted

1 teaspoon vanilla extract

1 cup cocoa powder

2 tablespoons butter

¼ cup caster sugar

½ cup chocolate syrup

2 cups milk

2 eggs

½ cup chocolate chips

Directions:

Beat eggs until fluffy.

In instant pot add butter and milk, leave to boil. Add cocoa powder and stir continuously.

Add caster sugar and eggs by stirring gradually.

Add melted chocolate and it mix thoroughly. Transfer into serving dish and place into the freezer for 20 minutes.

Drizzle chocolate syrup on top before serving.

UPSIDE DOWN PINEAPPLE CAKE

Preparation time: 10 minutes   Cooking time: 15 minutes   Servings: 4

Ingredients:

2 cups water

14oz. can pineapples, half sliced and half diced

¼ cup brown sugar

1 tablespoon butter

1 egg

1 cup ricotta cheese

1/3 cup sugar

3 tablespoons extra-virgin olive oil

1 cup all-purpose flour

1 teaspoon vanilla extract

1/8 teaspoon cinnamon powder

2 teaspoons baking powder

1 teaspoon baking soda

Directions:

Prepare the instant pot by adding 2 cups water and place the steamer basket inside.

In a greased cake tin sprinkle brown sugar equally along with butter.

Arrange pineapple slices in the bottom.

In a mixing bowl, mix egg, ricotta, sugar, olive oil, and vanilla extract.

Add flour, cinnamon powder, baking soda and baking powder.

Whisk all the ingredients together and stir in the diced pineapples.

Pour the batter into the prepared cake tin and place the tin into the steamer basket.

Turn the heat high and cook on high pressure for 15 minutes.

Open the lid using the natural release method.

Insert a toothpick in the middle of the cake to check for the doneness, a toothpick inserted should come out clean.

Turn the cake upside down on the wire rack, let it cook for several hours before serving.

$\mathcal{P}$OT BROWNIES

Preparation time: 5 minutes   Cooking time: 25 minutes   Servings: 8

Ingredients:

2 cups water for the Instant Pot
1 cup butter
1 egg
1/2 cup unsweetened cocoa powder
1 cup sugar

2/3 cup all-purpose flour
½ teaspoon vanilla paste
1 pinch salt
½ teaspoon baking soda
½ cup chopped walnuts

Directions:

Prepare the instant pot by adding 2 cups water and place the trivet inside pot.

Butter the sides and bottom of 9-inch spring form.

In a mixing bowl, combine egg, sugar, butter and vanilla extract.

Then add flour, cocoa powder, salt and baking powder. Fold in the walnuts.

Pour the batter into the prepared cake tin. Place this cake tin on the rack or metal trivet inside the Instant pot.

Turn the heat high and when the Pot reaches pressure, lower the heat to minimum. Cook for 25 minutes.

Open the lid using the natural release method. Insert a toothpick in the middle of the cake to check for the doneness, a toothpick inserted should come out clean.

Turn the brownie upside down on the wire rack let it cool for several hours. Slice and serve.

$\mathcal{P}$EANUT BUTTER BROWNIES

Preparation time: 5 minutes   Cooking time: 25 minutes   Servings: 8

Ingredients:

2 cups water, for the Instant Pot
½ cup butter
½ cup smooth peanut butter
1 egg
½ cup unsweetened cocoa powder
1 cup sugar

2/3 cup all-purpose flour
1 teaspoon vanilla extract
½ teaspoon baking powder
½ teaspoon salt
3 tablespoons roasted peanuts, crushed

Directions:

Prepare the instant pot by adding 2 cups water and place the trivet inside the pot.

Grease 9-inch springform pan with some butter.

In a mixing bowl, combine egg, sugar, butter, peanut butter and vanilla extract.
Add flour, cocoa powder, salt and baking powder.
Fold in the roasted peanuts and pour the batter into the prepared cake tin.
Place the cake tin on the trivet and cook on low pressure for 25 minutes.
Use a natural pressure release and open the lid. Check the doneness.
Remove the brownies from the pot and cool for few hours. Slice and serve.

STRAWBERRY RICOTTA CAKE

Preparation time: 5 minutes   Cooking time: 20 minutes   Servings: 6

Ingredients:

2 lb. ricotta cheese
4 eggs, beaten
1 cup strawberries, sliced or pureed
2 tablespoons olive oil

¼ cup honey
½ cup sugar
1 teaspoon vanilla paste
2 cups water

Directions:

Place a trivet in your Instant Pot and pour 2 cups of water in.
In a bowl, mix all the ingredients until the batter is smooth.
Place the batter into a heatproof dish, cover it with a foil and then place it on top the trivet.
Close the lid and select the "Multi-grain" function and "Adjust" down to 20 minutes.
Allow a natural release of 15 minutes.
Serve after.

APPLE BREAD PUDDING

Preparation time: 5 minutes   Cooking time: 10 minutes   Servings: 6

Ingredients:

1 cup melted butter
8 slices raisin bread
1 cup maple syrup
5 eggs

1 cup whipping cream
1 teaspoon vanilla extract
1 tablespoon cinnamon
1 cup apple sauce

Directions:

Grease an oven safe form that fits in instant pot with the butter.
In a bowl, combine the syrup, eggs, cream, cinnamon, applesauce, and vanilla.
Place the bread in the instant pot and pour the cream mixture over it.
Cover with tin foil. Set instant pot to high pressure and adjust the valve to manual.
Cook for 12 minutes and allow pressure to release on its own.
Serve with vanilla ice cream.

MILLET CREAM PUDDING

Preparation time: 5 minutes   Cooking time: 6 hours   Servings: 6

Ingredients:

1 cup melted butter
2 cups heavy cream
1 cup water
1 teaspoon vanilla extract

1 cup fresh strawberries
1 egg
1 cup maple syrup
1 cup millet flakes

Directions:

Fill your instant pot with all of the ingredients and stir well. Slow cook on the slow cook setting for 6-8 hours. Serve warm with some chopped mint.

BANANA BREAD PUDDING

Preparation time: 5 minutes   Cooking time: 12 minutes   Servings: 6

Ingredients:

1 cup melted butter
7 slices of bread
1 cup maple syrup
4 eggs

3 bananas, mashed
1 cup coconut cream
1 teaspoon vanilla extract

Directions:

Grease your heatproof dish and place into instant pot. In a bowl, combine the syrup, eggs, banana, cream and vanilla. Place the bread in the instant pot and pour the cream mixture over it. Cover with tin foil.
Set instant pot to high pressure and adjust the valve to manual. Cook for 12 minutes and allow pressure to release on its own. Serve with vanilla ice cream.

RASPBERRY RICOTTA CAKE

Preparation time: 5 minutes   Cooking time: 20 minutes   Servings: 4

Ingredients:

2 lb. ricotta cheese
4 eggs, beaten
1 cup raspberry puree
2 tablespoons olive oil

¼ cup honey
½ cup sugar
1 teaspoon vanilla paste
2 cups water

Directions:

Place a trivet in your Instant Pot and pour 2 cups of water in. In a bowl, mix all the ingredients until the batter is smooth. Place the batter into a heatproof dish, cover it with a foil and then place it on top the trivet.
Close the lid and select the "Multi-grain" function and "Adjust" down to 20 minutes.
Allow a natural release of 15 minutes. Serve after.

APPLE CRISP

Preparation time: 5 minutes   Cooking time: 6 hours   Servings: 8

Ingredients:

1 cup melted butter
2 cups coconut sugar
2 cups steel cut oats
1 teaspoon vanilla extract

1 egg
6 peeled and sliced apples
2 tablespoons cinnamon

Directions:

Fill your instant pot with all of the ingredients. Stir well.
Slow cook on the slow cook setting for 6-8 hours.
Serve warm.

APPLE CHEESECAKE

Preparation time: 5 minutes   Cooking time: 10 minutes   Servings: 6

Ingredients:

½ cup applesauce
4 cups cream cheese

3 eggs
1 teaspoon vanilla extract

Directions:

Grease a pie pan that fits in the instant pot with butter.
Mix the applesauce with the cream cheese, eggs, and vanilla. Place in the pie pan.
Cook on high pressure for 10 minutes.
Allow pressure valve to release on its own.
Allow to cool and serve garnished with cherries.

CHOCOLATE RICE PUDDING

Preparation time: 5 minutes   Cooking time: 25 minutes   Servings: 4

Ingredients:

1 cup rice
5 cups coconut milk
1 teaspoon vanilla extract
2 tablespoons cocoa powder

1 cup coconut sugar
1 tablespoon coconut oil
2 eggs, beaten

Directions:

Place all ingredients in the Instant Pot and press Saute.
Stir constantly and bring to a boil. Cover and seal, and press "Rice" button.
When rice program is finished, turn off and allow to sit for 15 minutes.
Stir and serve topped with strawberries or whipped cream.

PEACH CHEESECAKE

Preparation time: 5 minutes   Cooking time: 10 minutes   Servings: 6

Ingredients:

½ cup pureed peaches
4 cups cream cheese

3 eggs
1 teaspoon vanilla extract

Directions:

Grease a pie pan that fits in the instant pot with butter. Mix the peach puree with the cream cheese, eggs, and vanilla. Place in the pie pan. Cook on high pressure for 10 minutes. Allow pressure valve to release on its own. Allow to cool and serve garnished with cherries.

ALMOND CINNAMON COOKIES

Preparation time: 5 minutes   Cooking time: 10 minutes   Servings: 14 cookies

Ingredients:

1 ½ cups almond, flour
½ teaspoon baking soda
½ teaspoon cream of tartar
¼ teaspoon cinnamon

4 tablespoon butter
1 large egg
½ teaspoon vanilla
¼ cup stevia

Directions:

Spread a thick layer of sea salt at the bottom of the inner pot of your instant pot. Place in the trivet and add steaming basket. Preheat the instant pot on STEAM function for 10 minutes.
In a medium size bowl, mix all the ingredients and knead to make small balls.
Spray a 6-inch wide low baking pan with non-stick cooking spray.
Arrange and flatten the cookie balls about half an inch apart on baking pan.
Place the low baking pan in the instant pot on steaming basket.
Close, lock, and seal the valve. Raise the heat to HIGH and set the timer to 10 minutes.
Once done remove from the pot and place aside to cool completely. Serve after.

ALMOND SNOWBALLS

Preparation time: 10 minutes   Cooking time: 20 minutes   Servings: 18

Ingredients:

2 cups almond flour
1 cup walnuts
2 tablespoon coconut flour
1 teaspoon baking powder
1 teaspoon cardamom
¼ teaspoon salt

½ cup butter softened
½ cup brown sugar
1 large egg
1 teaspoon vanilla extract
¼ cup powdered sugar

Directions:

Spread a thick layer of sea salt at the bottom of the inner pot of your instant cooker. Place on the trivet.
Preheat the instant on SAUTE function for 15 minutes.
In a medium size bowl, mix all the ingredients except the powdered sugar. Shape the mixture into small bowls. Spray a 6-inch wide low baking pan with non-stick cooking spray.
Arrange and flatten the cookie balls about half an inch apart on baking pan.
Place the baking pan in the instant pot.
Raise the heat to HIGH and set the timer to 20 minutes.
When done, transfer the snowballs to a cooling rack; sprinkle powdered sugar over the cookie balls.
Serve when cooled completely.

SPICED APPLES

Preparation time: 5 minutes   Cooking time: 35 minutes   Servings: 4

Ingredients:

2 cups apple, peeled and diced
1 cup milk
½ cup brown sugar
½ teaspoon cinnamon powder

¼ teaspoon black pepper
4 tablespoons honey
1 pinch salt

Directions:

In a large bowl toss apples, cinnamon powder, black pepper, salt and transfer to instant pot.
Stir in milk, sugar, and cover with lid.
Let it cook for 35 minutes on slow cook mode. Put to serving the dish and drizzle honey on top.
Serve and enjoy.

PISTACHIO CAKE

Preparation time: 5 minutes   Cooking time: 45 minutes   Servings: 6

Ingredients:

2 tablespoons pistachio powder
4-5 tablespoons mint leaves, finely chopped
½ cup sugar
1 cup all-purpose flour

1 teaspoon vanilla extract
1 tablespoon cocoa powder
2 eggs
½ cup butter

Directions:

In a large bowl beat eggs until fluffy. In a separate bowl beat butter with sugar, add vanilla extract for 2 minutes. Add the butter mix to eggs and fold in the flour, vanilla extract, mint leaves, and pistachio powder.
Pour batter into greased instant pot and cover with lid.
Leave to cook on pressure cook mode for 45 minutes.
Serve and enjoy.

MIXED BERRIES CHEESECAKE

Preparation time: 5 minutes   Cooking time: 10 minutes   Servings: 6

Ingredients:

1 cup mixed berries, fresh or thawed
4 cups cream cheese

3 eggs
1 teaspoon vanilla extract

Directions:

Grease a pie pan that fits in the instant pot with butter. Mix the berries with the cream cheese, eggs, and vanilla. Place in the pie pan. Cook on high pressure for 10 minutes. Allow pressure valve to release on its own. Allow to cool and serve garnished with cherries.

BLUEBERRY JAM CAKE

Preparation time: 5 minutes   Cooking time: 20 minutes   Servings: 6

Ingredients:

16 oz. cream cheese
2 large eggs
2 teaspoons vanilla extract

½ cup sugar
1 cup blueberry jam

Directions:

Place all the ingredients except the blueberry jam in a blender. Blend until smooth in texture.
Transfer the mixture to a 7-inch springform pan; cover the pan with aluminum foil.
Place 2 cups of water into the inner pot of the instant pot; place the steamer basket in and gently place the tin pan on top of the steamer basket. Steam pressure for 20 minutes on HIGH.
Use the natural depressurizing technique.
Remove the tin pan from the instant pot and place aside to cool completely.
Chill in the fridge for 1 hour. Top with blueberry jam.

MACADAMIA CAKE

Preparation time: 5 minutes   Cooking time: 20 minutes   Servings: 10

Ingredients:

4 tablespoons butter
1 egg
2 tablespoons brown sugar

1 ½ cups almond flour, blanched
½ teaspoon baking soda
½ cup macadamia nuts, chopped

Directions:

Spray the bottom and sides of 6- inch round baking pan with cooking oil spray.
In a mixing bowl, combine all the ingredients except the chopped macadamia nuts.
Transfer the batter into the greased baking pan and evenly spread the mixture.

Top the batter with chopped macadamia nuts; cover the pan with aluminum foil.

Pour 2 cups of water in the inner pot of your instant pot; insert the trivet and place the baking pan on the trivet. Close the lid, lock, and seal the pressure cooker valve. Set the instant pot on STEAM on HIGH and cook for 20 minutes. When the time is up, release the pressure with the Quick release method. Transfer the cake to rack and once cooled serve.

*E*GG CUSTARD WITH FRUITS

Preparation time: 5 minutes   Cooking time: 15 minutes   Servings: 6

Ingredients:

6 egg yolks
4 grams sugar
2 cups heavy cream

1 tablespoon vanilla extract
Fresh fruits, like strawberries, blueberries, etc.

Directions:

Mix the egg yolks, sugar, cream and vanilla in a medium sized mixing bowl.

Gently pour the mixture into the ramekins through a sieve.

Cover the ramekins with foil. Pour 2 cups water in the instant pot and insert a trivet. Arrange ramekins on top.

Set your pressure cooker to STEAM function. Set the time to cook for 15 minutes.

Release the pressure the natural way, remove the ramekins, and transfer to a cooling rack.

Take off the tin foil and let cool for 30 minutes before transferring to the fridge to completely chill.

Serve topped with fresh fruits.

*C*ACAO CUSTARD

Preparation time: 5 minutes   Cooking time: 10 minutes   Servings: 4

Ingredients:

4oz. avocado
2 tablespoons cacao powder
2 tablespoon honey

½ cup coconut milk
½ teaspoon almond extract
1/8 teaspoon salt

1 tablespoon brown sugar

Directions:

Preheat the instant pot in STEAM mode, pour 2 cups of water and turn on the timer for 5 minutes.

In a blender, puree the avocado with the coconut milk and all ingredients except brown sugar.

Pour the pureed mixture into ramekins; cover the ramekins with aluminum tin foil.

Place the ramekins on top of your trivet and insert in the instant pot.

Close the lid, lock and seal the pressure cooker valve.

Cook on HIGH for 10 minutes. Do the Quick Release method to let out steam pressure.

Chill the custard for 1 hour. Sprinkle the custard with brown sugar and brown the sugar with a torch.

Serve after.

$\mathcal{B}$ROWNIE PUDDING

Preparation time: 5 minutes   Cooking time: 30 minutes   Servings: 6

Ingredients:

¾ cup cocoa powder, unsweetened
¼ cup flour
2 eggs
1 cup sugar

7 tablespoon melted butter
1 ½ cup water
¼ cup chocolate chips
½ teaspoon vanilla paste

Directions:

Prepare your Instant Pot by adding in some water and placing the steam rack on top.

Prepare the baking dish with a bit of butter.

Beat together the eggs and the sugar in a big bowl for a few minutes to make them fluffy.

In a separate bowl, whisk together the salt, cocoa powder, and flour until the lumps are gone.

Add in the egg and sugar mixture and then add in the rest of the butter and the vanilla and keep mixing until just combined.

Pour this into the baking dish and top with some chocolate chips.

Place into the Instant pot and secure the lid.

Cook the pudding for 30 minutes on a high pressure. Once this time is up, use the quick release option to let out the steam.

Take the pan out and let it cool down before slicing and serving.

$\mathcal{A}$PRICOT JAM CAKE

Preparation time: 5 minutes   Cooking time: 20 minutes   Servings: 6

Ingredients:

16 oz. cream cheese
2 large eggs
2 teaspoons vanilla extract

½ cup sugar
1 cup apricot jam
2 tablespoons crushed almonds, to sprinkle

Directions:

Place all the ingredients except the jam and almonds in a blender. Blend until smooth in texture.

Transfer the mixture to a 7-inch springform pan; cover the pan with aluminum foil.

Place 2 cups of water into the inner pot of the instant pot; place the steamer basket in and gently place the tin pan on top of the steamer basket.

Steam pressure for 20 minutes on HIGH.

Use the natural depressurizing technique.

Remove the tin pan from the instant pot and place aside to cool completely.

Chill in the fridge for 1 hour. Top with jam and almonds.

KEY LIME CHEESECAKE

Preparation time: 10 minutes   Cooking time: 15 minutes   Servings: 10

Ingredients:

½ cup graham cracker crumbs
3 tablespoons melted butter
1 ½ cup water
1 ½ tablespoons flour
½ teaspoon vanilla

1 teaspoon key lime zest
2 tablespoons key lime juice
2 eggs
½ cup sugar
1 lb. cream cheese

Directions:

In a bowl, combine 2 tablespoons of butter with the graham cracker crumbs.

Press the mixture down into a prepared baking pan and let it go up the sides a bit.

In another bowl, beat the sugar and cream cheese together to make smooth and creamy.

Add the vanilla, lime zest, and lime juice and stir well.

Add in the flour and beat well before pouring into your prepared crust.

Place some water in the Instant Pot, around 2 cups.

Insert trivet and place the cake onto the trivet. Lock the lid and cook for 15 minutes on a high pressure. When done, slowly release the pressure before taking the pie out.

Allow the cake to come to room temperature. Chill for 1 hour before slicing.

PEACH BERRY COBBLER

Preparation time: 10 minutes   Cooking time: 15 minutes   Servings: 6

Ingredients:

¼ teaspoon baking soda
½ teaspoon salt
1 ½ teaspoons baking powder
½ cup sugar
1 cup all-purpose flour
1 teaspoon lemon juice
1 tablespoon cornstarch

1/3 cup water
2 cups blueberries
2 cups peaches
1/3 cup buttermilk
2 tablespoons cubed butter, chilled
1 pinch nutmeg

Directions:

Take out a bowl and mix together the baking soda, salt, baking powder, flour, and 1 tablespoon sugar.

Add in the butter and use your hands to make a coarse meal.

Add the buttermilk just a bit at a time and stir.

Select the Saute option and add the peaches, water, blueberries, nutmeg, lemon juice, cornstarch, and the rest of the sugar. Cook this for 3 minutes

Tear off small balls of prepared dough and nestle it on the fruit. Place the lid back on the slow cooker and cook at a high pressure for 10 minutes.

Use the quick release method to release the lid and allow it to cool a few minutes before serving.

CRESCENT APPLE DUMPLINGS

Preparation time: 5 minutes   Cooking time: 10 minutes   Servings: 6

Ingredients:

4 tablespoons butter
1 apple, sliced in 8 pieces
1 can crescent rolls
¾ cup apple cider

1 pinch nutmeg
1 teaspoon cinnamon
½ teaspoon vanilla
½ cup brown sugar

Directions:

Preheat the Instant Pot by selecting Saute option.

Open the crescent rolls and roll it out flat.

Roll one piece of apple into each of the rolls.

Add in butter to the Pot and select Cancel.

Add the nutmeg, cinnamon, vanilla, and sugar. Place the dumplings inside the pot and drizzle the cider along the edges.

Select Manual and let it cook for 10 minutes on high pressure.

Use a quick pressure release and allow to cool before serving.

GINGER CRÈME BRULEE

Preparation time: 5 minutes   Cooking time: 10 minutes   Servings: 6

Ingredients:

2 cup heavy cream
¾ cup sugar
1 teaspoon vanilla paste

½ teaspoon minced ginger
4 egg yolks
1 cup warm water

Directions:

Mix all of the ingredients together except the warm water. Fill up four ramekin dishes and then wrap with aluminum foil.

Place your inner pot inside the pot and then pour a cup of water into the pot.

Insert the trivet and arrange ramekins onto the trivet. Lock the lid and cook on high pressure for 10 minutes.

Use a quick pressure release and remove the ramekins. Chill the crème Brulee for 1 hour.

Top with sugar before serving and caramelize the sugar, using a torch.

Serve and enjoy.

WHITE CHOCOLATE COOKIES

Preparation time: 10 minutes   Cooking time: 8 minutes   Servings: 12

Ingredients:

3 tablespoons milk

6oz. flour

1 tablespoon heavy cream

1 teaspoon baking powder

½ cup butter

3 eggs

2oz. white chocolate

5oz. sugar

2oz. melted dark chocolate

1 pinch salt

Directions:

Melt the white chocolate with heavy cream in microwave on high.

In a bowl, mix all the dry ingredients. In a separate bowl, beat the eggs with sugar until pale and fluffy.

Fold the dry ingredients into the egg mixture and add remaining ingredients, except the dark chocolate.

Place 2 cups water in instant pot and insert trivet. Shape the mixture into balls and arrange onto a baking dish, the one that can fit into your pot.

Flatten down the cookies and lock the lid. Cook on high pressure for 8 minutes. Remove from the pot and place aside to cool. Drizzle the cookies with melted dark chocolate just before serving.

CARAMEL FLAN

Preparation time: 10 minutes   Cooking time: 30 minutes   Servings: 6

Ingredients:

5 egg yolks

2 ½ cups milk

1 teaspoon vanilla paste

10 tablespoons sugar

Directions:

Pick out the flan mold that you would like. Place it your instant pot. Add in a bit of water and 4 tablespoons of sugar and then make the caramel.

In a pan boil the milk for about 10 minutes along with the vanilla.

Beat the egg yolks with remaining sugar.

Add in the milk and mix to get a cream that is even. Place the cream into the mold.

Pour 2 cups water into the instant pot. Close the lid and then cook for 30 minutes on Steam mode.

Use a quick pressure release and remove the molds. Chill the flan for 2 hours before serving.

ORANGE CHEESECAKE

Preparation time: 10 minutes   Cooking time: 15 minutes   Servings: 10

Ingredients:

½ cup graham cracker crumbs

3 tablespoons melted butter

1 ½ cup water

1 ½ tablespoons flour

½ teaspoon vanilla

1 teaspoon orange zest

2 tablespoons orange juice

2 eggs

½ cup sugar

1 lb. cream cheese

Directions:

In a bowl, combine 2 tablespoons of butter with the graham cracker crumbs.

Press the mixture down into a prepared baking pan and let it go up the sides a bit.

In another bowl, beat the sugar and cream cheese together to make smooth and creamy.

Add the vanilla, orange juice, orange zest, and stir well.

Add in the flour and beat well before pouring into your prepared crust.

Place some water in the Instant Pot, around 2 cups.

Insert trivet and place the cake onto the trivet. Lock the lid and cook for 15 minutes on a high pressure. When done, slowly release the pressure before taking the pie out.

Allow the cake to come to room temperature. Chill for 1 hour before slicing.

GRANNY'S PUDDING

Preparation time: 5 minutes   Cooking time: 20 minutes   Servings: 4

Ingredients:

2 cups milk

1 teaspoon vanilla paste

1 egg

3 tablespoons water

1 tablespoon sugar

1 tablespoon instant coffee

3 tablespoons condensed milk

Directions:

Beat the eggs in a bowl.

Add the milk and condensed milk and beat well. Add in the vanilla extract now. Continue to mix.

Turn on the Instant Pot and put it on "Sauté" for 5 minutes.

Put all of the ingredients into the Instant Pot and let it simmer for 4 minutes.

Close the lid. Put the Instant Pot on "Manual" and set it to 15 minutes.

Take out the contents and let them cool.

Serve after.

ANOTHER BROWNIE RECIPE

Preparation time: 10 minutes   Cooking time: 2 hours   Servings: 8

ingredients:

2 tablespoons cocoa powder

½ cup brown sugar

2 cups brownie mix

2 eggs

3 tablespoons melted butter

1 cup water

½ cup caramel chips

Directions:

Turn on the Instant Pot and set it on "Sauté" to get it heated. Let this run for 5 minutes.

Take out a separate bowl and add in the brownie mix, sugar, caramel chips, eggs, butter, and water.

Take out a cake pan and place these ingredients inside.

Put the cake pan into the Instant Pot and let it sit for 3 minutes.

Close the lid and put the Instant Pot on "Manual". You will set the timer to 2 hours.

Take out the cake dish and let it cool for 30 minutes.

Slice the cake and serve.

CHOCOLATE FONDUE

Preparation time: 5 minutes   Cooking time: 10 minutes   Servings: 12

Ingredients:

2lb. chopped Dark Chocolate
1 cup chopped strawberries
1 cup chopped pineapples

1 cup chopped bananas
2/3 cup evaporated milk
2 cups mini marshmallows

Directions:

Take out a mixing bowl and add the following ingredients marshmallows, milk, and dark chocolate. Mix well in order to have it evenly spread. Transfer into cake pan.

Turn on the Instant Pot and let it sit on "Sauté" for 5 minutes.

Put the cake pan into the Instant Pot and let it sit for 5 minutes. Close the lid and hit the "Manual". Heat for 10 minutes. Take out the pan and pour into a serving bowl. Serve with fruits.

PEAR RICOTTA CAKE

Preparation time: 5 minutes   Cooking time: 20 minutes   Servings: 4

Ingredients:

2 lb. ricotta cheese
4 eggs, beaten
2 Bosc pears, diced
2 tablespoons olive oil

¼ cup honey
½ cup sugar
1 teaspoon vanilla paste
2 cups water

Directions:

Place a trivet in your Instant Pot and pour 2 cups of water in.

1n a bowl, mix all the ingredients until the batter is smooth.

Place the batter into a heatproof dish, cover it with a foil and then place it on top the trivet.

Close the lid and select the "Multi-grain" function and "Adjust" down to 20 minutes.

Allow a natural release of 15 minutes.

Serve after.

BANANA CINNAMON PUDDING

Preparation time: 5 minutes   Cooking time: 8 minutes   Servings: 6

Ingredients:

1 teaspoon paste
1 teaspoon dark rum
1/2 cup sour cream
1/2 cup sweetened condensed milk
1/2 cup half-and-half

1 teaspoon cinnamon
tablespoons sugar
2 large egg yolks
1 egg
2 bananas

Directions

Add 2 cups of water to the Instant Pot and insert a steamer basket.

Puree the bananas in a blender or processor. Mix in the condensed milk, rum, eggs, and half, vanilla, cinnamon, and sour cream. Blend until smooth.

Transfer to a souffle dishes and transfer into the pot on the steamer basket.

Lock the lid, select Manual and cook for 8 minutes.

Let the pressure release naturally. Chill in the fridge before serving.

Banana Muffins

Preparation time: 5 minutes   Cooking time: 15 minutes   Servings: 4

Ingredients:

½ cup almond, flour
½ cup butter
1 medium banana
3 tablespoons milk, almond

1/8 teaspoon salt,
2 tablespoons sugar
1 teaspoon cinnamon

Directions:

Preheat your pressure cooker to the STEAM function. Add 2 cups of water.

Grease 4 muffin tin cups with butter. In a mixing bowl, combine all the ingredients and mix well.

Pour the egg-cream mixture into each greased muffin cup.

Arrange the muffin tin cups in your instant pot.

Steam for 15 minutes. Use a natural pressure release and open the lid.

Serve at room temperature.

Brazil Nuts Cookies

Preparation time: 5 minutes   Cooking time: 20 minutes   Servings: 16

Ingredients:

½ cup coconut oil
¼ cup butter, unsalted
2 teaspoons maple syrup

1 teaspoon almond extract
¼ teaspoon sea salt.
8oz. Brazil nuts, roasted

Directions:

Spread a thick layer of sea salt at the bottom of the inner pot of your instant pot. Place your trivet and steamer basket on top of the layer of sea salt. Preheat the pressure cooker on SAUTE function for 10 minutes. In a medium size bowl, mix all the ingredients and knead to make small balls.

Spray a 6-inch wide low baking pan with non-stick cooking spray.

Arrange and flatten the cookie balls about half an inch apart.

Place the low baking pan in the pot on a trivet.

Raise the heat to HIGH and set the timer to 20 minutes.

Loosely cover the pressure cooker with the lid.

APPLE RICOTTA CAKE

Preparation time: 5 minutes   Cooking time: 20 minutes   Servings: 4

Ingredients:

2 lb. ricotta cheese
4 eggs, beaten
2 apples, chopped
2 tablespoons olive oil

¼ cup honey
½ cup sugar
1 teaspoon vanilla paste
2 cups water

Directions:

Place a trivet in your Instant Pot and pour 2 cups of water in.
In a bowl, mix all the ingredients until the batter is smooth.
Place the batter into a heatproof dish, cover it with a foil and then place it on top the trivet.
Close the lid and select the "Multi-grain" function and "Adjust" down to 20 minutes.
Allow a natural release of 15 minutes.
Serve after.

TAPIOCA PUDDING

Preparation time: 5 minutes   Cooking time: 8 minutes   Servings: 4

Ingredients:

1 ¼ cups milk
1/3 cup tapioca pearls, rinsed
½ cup of sugar

½ cup of water
½ vanilla bean, seeds scraped out

Directions:

Place the steamer basket inside your instant pot and add one cup of water in order to get set up.
Use a heat-proof bowl that can hold at least 4 cups of liquid to add together the tapioca, milk, water, sugar, and vanilla seeds.
Mix well and place in the instant pot. Lock the lid and cook on high pressure for 8 minutes.
Release pressure naturally.
Serve pudding when reaches room temperature.

Yogurt recipes

MANGO YOGURT

Preparation time: 15 minutes   Cooking time: 14 hours   Servings: 4

Ingredients:

2 cans full cream milk
4 capsules high-quality probiotic
1 tbsp. raw honey

1 tsp. vanilla extract
2 tbsp. gelatine
1 cup mango puree or pulp

Directions:

Place the milk in instant pot.

Lock the lid and select the yogurt button, then press the adjust button till the display states boil.

When the Instant Pot beeps, turn off the pot, remove the lid and take out the metal bowl.

Using a candy thermometer measure the temperature of the milk till it reaches 115 C.

Once the milk is cooled below 115 C, empty the contents of probiotic capsules in the milk.

Stir in mango puree as well.

Return the metal bowl to the pot, close the lid and seal it and press the yogurt button again.

Use the (+) button to adjust the time to 14hours. When the Instant pot beeps, taste the yogurt to make sure it is tart.

Transfer the yogurt to the blender or food processor, sprinkle gelatin powder, add honey and vanilla extract. Blending the yogurt until smooth.

Pour the yogurt into glasses or bowls and refrigerate the same for 2-3 hours.

BLUEBERRY OATS YOGURT

Preparation time: 5 minutes   Cooking time: 14 hours   Servings: 6

Ingredients:

2 cans full cream milk
4 capsules high-quality probiotic
1 tablespoon raw honey
1 teaspoon vanilla paste

2 tablespoons gelatin powder
1/2 cup roasted oats
1 cup blueberry puree or pulp

Directions:

Place the milk in instant pot.

Lock the lid and select the yogurt button, then press the adjust button till the display states boil.

When the Instant Pot beeps, turn off the pot, remove the lid and take out the metal bowl.

Using a candy thermometer measure the temperature of the milk till it reaches 115 C.

Once the milk is cooled below 115 C, empty the contents of probiotic capsules in the milk.

Return the metal bowl to the pot, close the lid and seal it and press the yogurt button again.

Use the (+) button to adjust the time to 14hours. When the Instant pot beeps, taste the yogurt to make sure it is tart.

Transfer the yogurt to the blender or food processor, sprinkle gelatin powder and add remaining ingredients. Blending the yogurt in a food blender until smooth.

Pour the yogurt into glasses or bowls and refrigerate the same for 2-3 hours.

CINNAMON YOGURT

Preparation time: 5 minutes   Cooking time: 14 hours   Servings: 6

Ingredients:

2 cans full cream milk
4 capsules high-quality probiotic
1 tablespoon raw honey

1 teaspoon vanilla paste
2 tablespoons gelatin powder
2 teaspoons Ceylon cinnamon

Directions:

Place the milk in instant pot.

Lock the lid and select the yogurt button, then press the adjust button till the display states boil.

When the Instant Pot beeps, turn off the pot, remove the lid and take out the metal bowl.

Using a candy thermometer measure the temperature of the milk till it reaches 115 C.

Once the milk is cooled below 115 C, empty the contents of probiotic capsules in the milk.

Return the metal bowl to the pot, close the lid and seal it and press the yogurt button again.

Use the (+) button to adjust the time to 14hours. When the Instant pot beeps, taste the yogurt to make sure it is tart.

Transfer the yogurt to the blender or food processor, sprinkle gelatin powder and add remaining ingredients. Blending the yogurt in a food blender until smooth.

Pour the yogurt into glasses or bowls and refrigerate the same for 2-3 hours.

CHOCOLATE YOGURT

Preparation time: 5 minutes   Cooking time: 14 hours   Servings: 4

Ingredients:

2 cans full cream milk
4 capsules high-quality probiotic
1 tablespoon raw honey
1 teaspoon vanilla paste

2 tablespoons gelatin powder
2 tablespoons cocoa powder
1 cup melted dark chocolate

Directions:

Place the milk in instant pot. Add cocoa powder.

Lock the lid and select the yogurt button, then press the adjust button until the display states boil.

When the Instant Pot beeps, turn off the pot, remove the lid and take out the metal bowl.

Using a candy thermometer measure the temperature of the milk till it reaches 115 C.

Once the milk is cooled below 115 C, empty the contents of probiotic capsules in the milk.

Return the metal bowl to the pot, close the lid and seal it and press the yogurt button again.

Use the (+) button to adjust the time to 14hours. When the Instant pot beeps, taste the yogurt to make sure it is tart.

Transfer the yogurt to the blender or food processor, sprinkle gelatin powder and add remaining ingredients. Blending the yogurt in a food blender until smooth.

Pour the yogurt into glasses or bowls and refrigerate the same for 2-3 hours.

RASPBERRY YOGURT

Preparation time: 5 minutes   Cooking time: 14 hours   Servings: 6

Ingredients:

2 cans full cream milk
4 capsules high-quality probiotic
1 tablespoon raw honey

1 teaspoon vanilla paste
2 tablespoons gelatin powder
1 cup raspberry puree

Directions:

Place the milk in instant pot.

Lock the lid and select the yogurt button, then press the adjust button till the display states boil.

When the Instant Pot beeps, turn off the pot, remove the lid and take out the metal bowl.

Using a candy thermometer measure the temperature of the milk till it reaches 115 C.

Once the milk is cooled below 115 C, empty the contents of probiotic capsules in the milk.

Return the metal bowl to the pot, close the lid and seal it and press the yogurt button again.

Use the (+) button to adjust the time to 14hours. When the Instant pot beeps, taste the yogurt to make sure it is tart.

Transfer the yogurt to the blender or food processor, sprinkle gelatin powder and add remaining ingredients. Blending the yogurt in a food blender until smooth.

Pour the yogurt into glasses or bowls and refrigerate the same for 2-3 hours.

STRAWBERRY YOGURT

Preparation time: 5 minutes   Cooking time: 14 hours   Servings: 4

Ingredients:

2 cans full cream milk
4 capsules high-quality probiotic
1 tablespoon raw honey

1 teaspoon vanilla paste
2 tablespoons gelatin powder
1 cup strawberry puree

Directions:

Place the milk in instant pot.

Lock the lid and select the yogurt button, then press the adjust button till the display states boil.

When the Instant Pot beeps, turn off the pot, remove the lid and take out the metal bowl.

Using a candy thermometer measure the temperature of the milk till it reaches 115 C.

Once the milk is cooled below 115 C, empty the contents of probiotic capsules in the milk.

Return the metal bowl to the pot, close the lid and seal it and press the yogurt button again.

Use the (+) button to adjust the time to 14hours. When the Instant pot beeps, taste the yogurt to make sure it is tart.

Transfer the yogurt to the blender or food processor, sprinkle gelatin powder and add remaining ingredients. Blending the yogurt in a food blender until smooth.

Pour the yogurt into glasses or bowls and refrigerate the same for 2-3 hours.

WHITE CHOCOLATE YOGURT

Preparation time: 5 minutes   Cooking time: 14 hours   Servings: 4

Ingredients:

2 cans full cream milk
4 capsules high-quality probiotic
1 tablespoon raw honey

1 teaspoon vanilla paste
2 tablespoons gelatin powder
1 cup melted white chocolate

Directions:

Place the milk in instant pot.

Lock the lid and select the yogurt button, then press the adjust button till the display states boil.

When the Instant Pot beeps, turn off the pot, remove the lid and take out the metal bowl.

Using a candy thermometer measure the temperature of the milk till it reaches 115 C.

Once the milk is cooled below 115 C, empty the contents of probiotic capsules in the milk.

Return the metal bowl to the pot, close the lid and seal it and press the yogurt button again.

Use the (+) button to adjust the time to 14hours. When the Instant pot beeps, taste the yogurt to make sure it is tart.

Transfer the yogurt to the blender or food processor, sprinkle gelatin powder, and add remaining ingredients, including white chocolate.

Blending the yogurt in a food blender until smooth.

Pour the yogurt into glasses or bowls and refrigerate the same for 2-3 hours.

PASSIONFRUIT YOGURT

Preparation time: 5 minutes   Cooking time: 14 hours   Servings: 4

Ingredients:

2 cans full cream milk
4 capsules high-quality probiotic
1 tablespoon raw honey

1 teaspoon vanilla paste
2 tablespoons gelatin powder
1 ½ cups passionfruit pulp

Directions:

Place the milk in instant pot.

Lock the lid and select the yogurt button, then press the adjust button till the display states boil.

When the Instant Pot beeps, turn off the pot, remove the lid and take out the metal bowl.

Using a candy thermometer measure the temperature of the milk till it reaches 115 C.

Once the milk is cooled below 115 C, empty the contents of probiotic capsules in the milk.

Return the metal bowl to the pot, close the lid and seal it and press the yogurt button again.

Use the (+) button to adjust the time to 14hours. When the Instant pot beeps, taste the yogurt to make sure it is tart.

Transfer the yogurt to the blender or food processor, sprinkle gelatin powder, and add remaining ingredients, including pulp.

Blending the yogurt in a food blender until smooth.

Pour the yogurt into glasses or bowls and refrigerate the same for 2-3 hours.

$\mathcal{P}$UMPKIN SPICE YOGURT

Preparation time: 5 minutes   Cooking time: 14 hours   Servings: 4

Ingredients:

2 cans full cream milk
4 capsules high-quality probiotic
1 tablespoon raw honey

1 teaspoon vanilla paste
2 tablespoons gelatin powder
1 tablespoon pumpkin spice

Directions:

Place the milk in instant pot.

Lock the lid and select the yogurt button, then press the adjust button till the display states boil.

When the Instant Pot beeps, turn off the pot, remove the lid and take out the metal bowl.

Using a candy thermometer measure the temperature of the milk till it reaches 115 C.

Once the milk is cooled below 115 C, empty the contents of probiotic capsules in the milk.

Return the metal bowl to the pot, close the lid and seal it and press the yogurt button again.

Use the (+) button to adjust the time to 14hours. When the Instant pot beeps, taste the yogurt to make sure it is tart.

Transfer the yogurt to the blender or food processor, sprinkle gelatin powder and add remaining ingredients.

Blending the yogurt in a food blender until smooth.

Pour the yogurt into glasses or bowls and refrigerate the same for 2-3 hours.

$\mathcal{V}$ANILLA YOGURT

Preparation time: 5 minutes   Cooking time: 14 hours   Servings: 4

Ingredients:

2 cans full cream milk
4 capsules high-quality probiotic
1 tablespoon raw honey

3 teaspoons vanilla paste
2 tablespoons gelatin powder

Directions:

Place the milk in instant pot.

Lock the lid and select the yogurt button, then press the adjust button till the display states boil.

When the Instant Pot beeps, turn off the pot, remove the lid and take out the metal bowl.

Using a candy thermometer measure the temperature of the milk till it reaches 115 C.

Once the milk is cooled below 115 C, empty the contents of probiotic capsules in the milk.

Return the metal bowl to the pot, close the lid and seal it and press the yogurt button again.

Use the (+) button to adjust the time to 14hours. When the Instant pot beeps, taste the yogurt to make sure it is tart.

Transfer the yogurt to the blender or food processor, sprinkle gelatin powder and add remaining ingredients.

Blending the yogurt in a food blender until smooth.

Pour the yogurt into glasses or bowls and refrigerate the same for 2-3 hours.

*K*IWI YOGURT

Preparation time: 5 minutes   Cooking time: 14 hours   Servings: 4

Ingredients:

2 cans full cream milk
4 capsules high-quality probiotic
1 tablespoon raw honey

1 teaspoon vanilla paste
2 tablespoons gelatin powder
¾ cup kiwi puree

Directions:

Place the milk in instant pot.

Lock the lid and select the yogurt button, then press the adjust button till the display states boil.

When the Instant Pot beeps, turn off the pot, remove the lid and take out the metal bowl.

Using a candy thermometer measure the temperature of the milk till it reaches 115 C.

Once the milk is cooled below 115 C, empty the contents of probiotic capsules in the milk.

Return the metal bowl to the pot, close the lid and seal it and press the yogurt button again.

Use the (+) button to adjust the time to 14hours. When the Instant pot beeps, taste the yogurt to make sure it is tart.

Transfer the yogurt to the blender or food processor, sprinkle gelatin powder and add remaining ingredients.

Blending the yogurt in a food blender until smooth.

Pour the yogurt into glasses or bowls and refrigerate the same for 2-3 hours.

Sauces

TOMATO SAUCE

Preparation time: 5 minutes   Cooking time: 6 hours   Servings: 4 cups

Ingredients:

2 cups tomato paste
2 tomatoes, chopped
1 cup sun-dried tomatoes, chopped
1/2 cup apple cider vinegar

1 tablespoon honey
3 cloves garlic, chopped
1 onion chopped.

Directions:

Place the ingredients in the instant pot. Slow cook for 6-8 hours.
Serve with pasta or rice.

CHILI TOMATO SAUCE

Preparation time: 5 minutes   Cooking time: 6 hours   Servings: 4 cups

Ingredients:

2 cups tomato paste
2 tomatoes, chopped
3 chili peppers, chopped
1 cup sun-dried tomatoes, chopped

1/2 cup apple cider vinegar
1 tablespoon honey
3 cloves garlic, chopped
1 onion chopped.

Directions:

Place the ingredients in the instant pot. Slow cook for 6-8 hours.
Serve with pasta or rice.

BASIL TOMATO SAUCE

Preparation time: 5 minutes   Cooking time: 6 hours   Servings: 4 cups

Ingredients:

2 cups tomato paste
1 cup basil leaves, chopped
2 tomatoes, chopped
1 cup sun-dried tomatoes, chopped

1/2 cup apple cider vinegar
1 tablespoon honey
3 cloves garlic, chopped
1 onion chopped.

Directions:

Place the ingredients in the instant pot. Slow cook for 6-8 hours.
Serve with pasta or rice.

CHEESE SAUCE

Preparation time: 5 minutes　　　Cooking time: 8 minutes　　　Servings: 4 cups

Ingredients:

1 cup chicken broth
1 cup cream cheese

2 cups cheddar cheese
1 tablespoon garlic powder

Directions:

Place the ingredients in the instant pot. Use the "warm" setting and warm for 8 minutes. Serve after.

CHILI CHEESE SAUCE

Preparation time: 5 minutes　　　Cooking time: 8 minutes　　　Servings: 4 cups

Ingredients:

1 cup chicken broth
1 cup cream cheese
2 cups cheddar cheese

1 tablespoon garlic powder
1 tablespoon chili powder

Directions:

Place the ingredients in the instant pot. Use the "warm" setting and warm for 8 minutes. Serve after.

ONION CHEESE SAUCE

Preparation time: 5 minutes　　　Cooking time: 8 minutes　　　Servings: 4 cups

Ingredients:

1 cup chicken broth
1 cup cream cheese

2 cups cheddar cheese
1 tablespoon onion powder

Directions:

Place the ingredients in the instant pot. Use the "warm" setting and warm for 8 minutes. Serve after.

BROCCOLI CREAM SAUCE

Preparation time: 5 minutes　　　Cooking time: 8 minutes　　　Servings: 4 cups

Ingredients:

1 cup chicken broth
1cup cream cheese
2 cups cheddar cheese

1 tablespoon garlic powder
1 cup broccoli
2 teaspoons black pepper

Directions:

Place all ingredients in instant pot. Use the "warm" setting and warm for 8 minutes. Serve with chips.

CAULIFLOWER CREAM SAUCE

Preparation time: 5 minutes   Cooking time: 8 minutes   Servings: 4 cups

Ingredients:

1 cup chicken broth
1cup cream cheese
2 cups cheddar cheese

1 tablespoon garlic powder
1 cup cauliflower florets, chopped
2 teaspoons black pepper

Directions:

Place all ingredients in instant pot. Use the "warm" setting and warm for 8 minutes. Serve with chips.

CARROT COCONUT SAUCE

Preparation time: 5 minutes   Cooking time: 8 minutes   Servings: 4 cups

Ingredients:

1 cup coconut milk
1 cup cream cheese
2 cups Swiss cheese, grated

1 tablespoon garlic powder
1 cup shredded carrots

Directions:

Place all ingredients in instant pot. Use the "warm" setting and warm for 8 minutes. Serve with noodles.

SCALLION SAUCE

Preparation time: 5 minutes   Cooking time: 8 minutes   Servings: 4 cups

Ingredients:

1 cup chicken broth
1 cup cream cheese

2 cups Swiss cheese, grated
1/2 cup chopped scallions

Directions:

Place the ingredients in the instant pot. Use the "warm" setting and warm for 8 minutes. Serve with chips.

DELIGHTFUL ONION SAUCE

Preparation time: 5 minutes   Cooking time: 8 minutes   Servings: 4 cups

Ingredients:

1cup vegetable broth
2 cups cream cheese

2 tablespoons onion powder
1chopped yellow onion

Directions:

Place the ingredients in the instant pot. Use the "warm" setting and warm for 8 minutes. Serve with vegetables.

PEPPER SAUCE

Preparation time: 5 minutes   Cooking time: 6 hours   Servings: 4 cups

Ingredients:

1 cup vegetable broth
2cups chopped red bell pepper
1 tablespoon paprika
1 cup sun dried tomatoes, chopped

1/2 cup apple cider vinegar
1 tablespoon honey
3 cloves garlic, chopped
1 onion, chopped

Directions:

Place the ingredients in the instant pot.
Slow cook for 6-8 hours.
Serve with pasta or rice.

ONION PARSLEY CHEESE SAUCE

Preparation time: 5 minutes   Cooking time: 8 minutes   Servings: 4 cups

Ingredients:

1 cup chicken broth
1 cup cream cheese
2 cups cheddar cheese

1 tablespoon onion powder
1 tablespoon dried parsley

Directions:

Place the ingredients in the instant pot.
Use the "warm" setting and warm for 8 minutes.
Serve after.

BASIL SAUCE

Preparation time: 5 minutes   Cooking time: 8 minutes   Servings: 2 cups

Ingredients:

1 cup cream cheese
2 cups fresh basil, chopped
1 tablespoon parmesan

2 tablespoons Parmesan, grated
2 tablespoons olive oil

Directions:

Place the ingredients in the instant pot.
Use the "warm" setting and warm for 8 minutes.
Serve after.

Tomato Goat Cheese Sauce

Preparation time: 5 minutes   Cooking time: 6 hours   Servings: 4 cups

Ingredients:

2 cups tomato paste
2tomatoes, chopped
1 cup sun-dried tomatoes, chopped
1/2 cup apple cider vinegar
1 tablespoon honey

3 cloves garlic, chopped
1 onion chopped
1 cup goat cheese
1 tablespoon parmesan cheese
1/2 cup mozzarella cheese

Directions:

Place the ingredients in the instant pot.
Slow cook for 6-8 hours.
Serve with pasta.

Coconut Sauce

Preparation time: 5 minutes   Cooking time: 8 minutes   Servings: 2 cups

Ingredients:

1 cup butter, melted
1 tablespoon garlic powder

1 cup coconut cream

Directions:

Place the ingredients in the instant pot. Use the "warm" setting and warm for 8 minutes. Serve after.

Dulce de Leche Sauce

Preparation time: 5 minutes   Cooking time: 40 minutes   Servings: 6

Ingredients:

16 cups water

1 can of condensed milk, sweetened

Directions:

In the Instant Pot, put a trivet and then position a can of condensed milk firmly on top. Ensure that it doesn't touch the side or the base of your cooker.
Add the water in order to cover the can until it is submerged.
Now lock the lid and Choose the "Soup" function and "Adjust" up to 40 minutes.
Carefully do a quick release when the timer is up.
Use tongs or some other handy kitchen utensil to take the can out.
Place the can on a heatproof surface at room temperature.
Once cold enjoy.

CONCLUSION

Sadly, we have now reached the end of the book, but you are about to begin a new journey in your kitchen with Instant pot.

We hope this book will make your life easier and give you a lot of ideas on how to prepare your breakfast, lunch, or dinner. But do not stop there; you can easily combine different types of recipes to create really gourmet daily menus.

Cook is an art and the Instant pot is amazing appliance that will assist you while creating the most delicious and nutritious pieces of art in your own kitchen.

The instant pot is not just another kitchen appliance, but, an appliance that saves your time and money, while providing amazing food that actually has valuable nutritional values.

Once you get used to preparing the food in the instant pot it will become your No1. kitchen tool. The food preparation with instant pot will become easier and you are likely to see some impressive results which will ultimately lead to a healthier, slimmer and happier you all because the food prepared in this appliance retain its natural values that are good for your health.